TRUE CRIME STORIES OF
EASTERN NORTH CAROLINA

TRUE CRIME STORIES OF EASTERN NORTH CAROLINA

Cathy Pickens

THE
History
PRESS

Published by The History Press
Charleston, SC
www.historypress.com

First published 2020

Manufactured in the United States

ISBN 9781467145114

Library of Congress Control Number: 2020930463

Notice: The information in this book is true and complete to the best of our knowledge. It is offered without guarantee on the part of the author or The History Press. The author and The History Press disclaim all liability in connection with the use of this book.

For those with stories to tell…

Of course we visited it, and came away as wise as most people do who go and gaze upon such mementoes of the past when in an unreflective mood.

—Mark Twain in Roughing It,
on visiting the spot where Captain Cook was killed

CONTENTS

Acknowledgements   11
Welcome   13

Black Widow I   17
Undetermined   31
The Missing and the Missed   45
Black Widow II   63
Bad Science   73
The Rockingham Murders   89
Swamp Outlaws   107
Unprecedented   113
Online Swingers and a Shooter   127
The Poisoners   137
Side Trips, Crime Bits and Oddities   157

References   165
About the Author   175

ACKNOWLEDGEMENTS

This book—and so many other wonderful things in my life—wouldn't have happened without other writers, researchers, librarians, journalists and those who've investigated and preserved these stories. Special thanks go to Suzanne Barr, Paula Connolly, Dawn Cotter, Libby Dickinson, Bob Finley, Terry Hoover, John Jeter, Charles Oldham and Ann Wicker, for helping preserve and tell these stories.

WELCOME

North Carolina's first settlers—the Lost Colony—created its first mystery, a mystery that seems at odds with the lush beauty of Roanoke Island and the Outer Banks. The juxtaposition of dense forests and beautiful beaches with high dunes, charming seacoast towns and massive military bases, small towns and swamps—those classic images of Eastern North Carolina all provide backdrops for an equally wide-ranging array of mysteries and murders.

Cross the tidal marshes and wide sounds and inlets and move inland along the black-water rivers with names familiar because hurricanes and devastating floods always make headlines: Neuse, Tar, Lumber, Cape Fear and more. Between the rivers, find quintessential rural and small-town life—towns with main streets lined with churches, boarded-up storefronts and shuttered factories; tidy homes; pine forests; and green landscapes with fields full of corn, soybeans and tobacco.

Eastern North Carolina is a land of contrasts: beautiful and bleak, peaceful and stormy, quiet and howling. Those contrasts are also evident in the region's crime stories.

Why These Cases?

These stories start in Southport, at the lower end of the Outer Banks, with a well-traveled black widow and a tragic, still unexplained death at the foot

Dune-lined beach. *Photo by Anton Sharov on Unsplash.com.*

of Bald Head Island Lighthouse. The trail zigzags up the coast and farther inland, covering cases well known and those whose details have begun to fade from most memories.

A lovelorn war hero or a stalker? A cruel, conniving wife. A man released from one Death Row only to be sentenced to another. A duo of poisoning cases, more than one hundred years apart. A band of folk hero swamp outlaws. Sex swingers, a couple of mummies and an assortment of quirky cases. Each story has, in its way, helped define Eastern North Carolina and its history.

My family has been in the Carolinas for more than three hundred years, steeped in southern storytelling. Because any retelling of stories naturally depends on the storyteller's choices, these Eastern North Carolina stories are those that, for one reason or another, captured my imagination.

This book is not a work of investigative journalism. The information is drawn solely from published or broadcast resources, including newspapers, television documentaries, podcasts, books, print and online magazine articles and scholarly papers.

Longleaf pines and wiregrass forest, Fort Bragg. *Courtesy of Library of Congress.*

A New and Accurate Map of North Carolina (1779) of Eastern North Carolina counties. *Courtesy of Lionel Pincus and Princess Firyal Map Division, New York Public Library Digital Collections, accessed August 27, 2019. http://digitalcollections.nypl.org/items/9e44cc40-3e4c-0135-f362-13b5543211e9.*

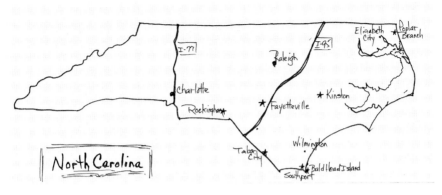

Map of Eastern North Carolina cases. *Sketch by Cathy Pickens.*

One of the handicaps in recounting historical events is that accounts vary. Some reported "facts" aren't accurate, or they are at odds with someone else's memory or perception of the event. While I have worked to dig out as many points of view as possible, I'm sure there are mistakes. My apologies in advance.

For me, senseless crime and violence do not make for fascinating stories. What fascinates is not random violence but rather the people and their lives. Some of these stories could have happened anywhere. Some made huge headlines far away from Eastern North Carolina. Others remain writ large only in the hearts of family and friends of those involved. Some take detours far from North Carolina because that's where the story went, but they all come home again. All of them, woven together, demonstrate the importance of family and home in this land and the people drawn to it.

Welcome to Eastern North Carolina and its crime stories.

BLACK WIDOW I

Brunswick County

On a movie screen, the life of a con artist looks glamorous. It looks like Leonardo DiCaprio donning a dashing airline pilot's uniform or playing at being a doctor to impress beautiful women. It's *Ocean's Eleven* pulling a heist with humor and high tension or handsome Robin Hood stealing from the rich.

In reality, the life of a con man (or woman) is best reflected in the pain and embarrassment of the victims: The man who withdrew $70,000 from his retirement account to help out a lonely widow until her trust fund could reimburse him. The tall, athletic former basketball player or the successful dentist who ran up huge debts satisfying a southern belle's lifestyle. Movies rarely portray the humiliation of falling for brazen, unbelievable lies—that deep gut ache of realization: *You've been duped. Your finances are in shambles, you're in trouble and you're ashamed. How could you have been so stupid?*

Looking through the victims' eyes, anyone could feel the frisson of fear. Could I be that foolish? What if I met the person who could prey on my weaknesses or generosity? Someone who needed my help, who gave me little space to say no? Could it happen to me?

Telling such a tale from the viewpoint of the con artist is difficult. How do you believably portray a mind that doesn't work like other minds? How do you explain someone who lives only by taking advantage of others, without regard for the damage left in the wake?

Historic marker at Southport's tree-shaded waterfront park. *Photo by Cathy Pickens.*

Are con artists motivated by greed? By a deep-seated insecurity grown in a childhood of upheaval and uncertainty? Or do they just enjoy the game, being smarter than everyone else, seeing how far they can play it before they move on to the next mark, oblivious or uncaring about the pain they create?

As with any state, North Carolina has a history of homegrown con artists, most of them men. But in 2006, a woman arrived in Southport, population about 2,500, trailing suspicions of murder and financial misdeeds from Texas to California, through Boston, Connecticut, Hawaii, Tucson, Atlanta and perhaps other places. She'd been adopted as a child, raised in the Oak Cliff suburb of Dallas. Her adoptive mother died when she was only three—not that any of that explains what came later.

The Texas Years

In her early sixties, Sandra Camille Powers Stegall Bridewell Rehrig Dandridge surfaced in Southport. The town's website identifies it as "the home of salubrious breezes," meaning "favorable to or promoting health or well-being." Southport is a gracious seacoast town, south of Wilmington and across the Cape Fear River from Bald Head Island. With its quaint downtown, expansive water views and canopy of gnarled live oaks, Southport has served as filming site for dozens of movies, including *Weekend at Bernie's*, *Crimes of the Heart* and Nicholas Sparks's *Safe Haven*, and television shows including Stephen King's *Under the Dome* and *Dawson's Creek*.

Sandra Bridewell's introductions in Southport came from a former preacher she met as she stood outside a grocery store, with bags at her feet, looking disheveled. Through the preacher's connections, she eventually found a home as a caregiver for Sue Moseley in a gated Southport community, a long way from where Sandra started.

Sandra, who was using her maiden name Camille Powers, told folks that she'd attended Texas Christian University (TCU) and Southern Methodist University (SMU), but in reality, she'd dropped out of Tyler Junior College after one year and set about her choice of career: finding a rich Dallas husband. She succeeded nicely.

She had been living the young, single career life in Dallas when she met David Stegall, a handsome, studious dental student living in the apartment across the way. In 1967, they married. Both the dentist and his young wife wanted to be rich, and he needed a practice that did more than simple cleanings and fillings, so Stegall studied with a Hollywood dentist to learn how to build a successful practice, what services to offer and how to meet potential clients. She focused on cooking, entertaining, decorating and buying antiques, building for them an enviable lifestyle. Together, they had three children.

Unfortunately, their lush life floated on a sea of debt. By most reports, they both enjoyed spending money, and by 1974, debts were swamping them. According to *D Magazine*'s in-depth 1987 report, Dr. Stegall consulted a psychologist, who said that Stegall was "pretty put out" by the bills for redecorating, added to the tax lien and the money he'd had to borrow from his father, but his wife "seemed to have him in a very painful box. He was completely intimidated by her."

In February 1975, Sandra called her husband's friend and lawyer, frantic. David had been drinking too much. When the attorney came over, the

Old Brunswick County Jail in Southport, in use from 1904 to 1971. *Photo by Cathy Pickens.*

two found David hiding in a closet, holding a gun against his temple. He got David to surrender the gun before he harmed himself. Within a few weeks, however, Sandra found David dead in the bed, both wrists slit and a .22-caliber wound in his head.

His death left Sandra adrift. With the proceeds from his life insurance, from selling their Greenway Parks house and from his dental practice, she was able to pay their debts and still have enough to support the family. Reports say that she was a good mother, devoted to her children.

She was also a woman who preferred having a rich husband around, and she knew where in Dallas to go hunting. Apparently, she also had the skills. More than one friend described her as feminine, her large dark eyes as "sparkling," her gaze as "intense" and her manner as "flirtatious." Descriptions of encounters with Sandra over the years, when she was scouting for husbands or, later, for fraud victims, were consistent: she looked slender or frail, which invited people to help her. "She had a way," they said, a hard-to-define "something" that was alluring. Sandra undoubtedly had that "something," especially in her younger years. Sandra dated a lot after

David's death, including a drama-fraught time with the founder of the Steak and Ale restaurant chain in the midst of his tense divorce.

About three years after her first husband's death, in June 1978, Sandra married Dallas developer Bobby Bridewell. He adopted her son and two daughters, and they moved to her dream neighborhood: Highland Park.

Highland Park sat north of central Dallas, with a population of nine thousand by 1980. Highland Park was a place where people grew up and stayed—or, if they weren't lucky enough to start life there, where they hoped to move as soon as they could. Part of the Park Cities area, home to Southern Methodist University and the Dallas Country Club, Highland Park was one of the wealthiest addresses in Texas.

Bobby Bridewell enjoyed the horse races and his good-time reputation, and Sandra fit herself easily into his fun-filled lifestyle. Real estate development has booms and busts, though, especially in Texas, where the economy floats on the price of oil. In 1978, Bobby Bridewell declared bankruptcy, with a reported $3 million in debt.

What busts can eventually boom again, if you're as creative and energetic as Bobby. In 1979, he hit on the idea for one of his most iconic hotel development projects: the Mansion Hotel on Turtle Creek, centered on a sprawling 1920s mansion in Highland Park, opulent even by Dallas standards. When the hotel opened in 1980, Bobby was back in the black, supporting their lavish life.

The picture painted of their marriage was a happy one. She called him her soul mate. They were both involved with their children's lives. If things had run a storybook course, Sandra Bridewell's name would have appeared only in the Dallas society pages. But tragedy struck the poor newly rich girl a cruel blow. In 1980, soon after prosperity returned, Bobby Bridewell was diagnosed with lymphatic cancer. He died two years later, in May 1982.

During his cancer battle, the gossip common to most closed communities began to dissect Sandra and her actions. Some felt that redecorating their home was in poor taste—costing money and disrupting Bobby's place of refuge. Others poo-poohed the naysayers. They'd been redecorating the house before he fell ill—Sandra was just finishing the work. Battle lines began to form, for and against Sandra. Over distance and time, the precise reasons are difficult, even impossible to discern.

During the cancer fight, Sandra came to rely on Bobby's oncologist, Dr. John Bagwell, and his wife, Betsy, for friendship and support. When Bobby died, her demands on the Bagwells intensified. Was she lonely and in need of emotional support? She considered Betsy a good friend. Or did she have designs on the accomplished oncologist? The story depended on who was bearing the gossip.

In July, Sandra phoned John Bagwell; her car had died and she needed a lift. As he arrived, he saw a policeman slide into the front seat and start her car right up. That was the last straw for the physician, tired of her machinations.

Soon after, when investigators started asking questions of those around Sandra, they found discrepancies in Sandra's stories, details preserved in police, private investigator and later journalist reports. Dr. Bagwell told investigators he felt Sandra lied about her car trouble to get him out of the house, away from his family.

Betsy Bagwell, though, continued to feel compassion. She listened the day Sandra called to tell her about a letter she'd found suggesting Bobby had been having an affair. Betsy asked friends lunching that day at the Dallas Country Club if anyone thought it possible Bobby could have been unfaithful. Hard to believe of him, they said. That same afternoon, Sandra called again with more car trouble. Betsy left her dinner fixings thawing in the sink, left instructions for her children not to ruin their appetites and went to drive Sandra to Love Field Airport to get a rental car.

At 8:20 p.m. on that July 16 evening, Betsy was found in the front seat of her late-model pale-blue Mercedes wagon, a bullet hole in her right temple and a stolen Saturday Night Special .22 in her hand. She left no suicide note. As far as anyone knew, she had intended to come home after her errand of aid and cook dinner for her family; she had no known upheavals in her life. But she had gunshot residue on her hand, in what the Dallas medical examiner called "a classic textbook case of suicide." No public report at the time raised the issue that gunshot residue, especially from a cheap handgun, can scatter broadly. Residue also could deposit on her hand if she reached to push away the barrel.

Doubting the official police solution, the family hired a private investigator. The gun had been stolen from a car years earlier in Dallas's Oak Cliff neighborhood—coincidentally, the one where Sandra grew up. Guns were easy to buy in Texas gun shops in the 1980s, even in expensive parts of town. But where would a Dallas doctor's wife get a cheap stolen handgun? Despite the questions, the official ruling of suicide couldn't be disproved.

The rumor mill ground into fine powder all manner of gossip, and neighbors drew their own conclusions and their own alliances. One neighbor told a reporter that people "grew wary of Sandra," wondering what was real and what was safe to believe. Sandra's children began to face the redrawn loyalty lines in their posh, small town–like neighborhood.

Meanwhile, Sandra bought herself a sporty new Mercedes and, with memorial donations for Bobby, started a summer camp for children with cancer.

Sandra was also back in the dating game, but her next catch simply stopped his Ford Bronco in front of her house on a whim. In the summer of 1984, she was still living in Highland Park when a tall twenty-nine-year-old described as "all-American cute" flagged her down in her front yard and asked if she knew of any garage apartments for rent in the area. Alan Rehrig, a former Oklahoma State basketball and football player, was newly arrived in Dallas, starting a job at a friend's mortgage company after a short stint as a professional golfer. His $24,000 salary wouldn't buy much, but he knew Highland Park would be a nice start, even in a garage apartment.

Six months later, athletic Alan Rehrig and delicate southern belle Sandra Bridewell were married at her second husband's Turtle Creek luxury hotel. Alan, raised in a Christian home in Edmond, Oklahoma, had a good ol' boy manner and was taken by the attentions of the sophisticated older beauty. He didn't know how much older, as Sandra claimed she was six years his senior, lying about the eleven-year gap. After five months of dating, he also believed her when she told him she was pregnant. He did what nice boys from Oklahoma do, even though he didn't feel ready to commit to a marriage or children.

He and his friends enjoyed her premium seats at the Dallas Mavericks games (tickets she said came from her deceased husband but which she really bought from a scalper), but he was surprised at her fussiness, refusing a hot dog at an Oklahoma State football tailgate. Some of her friends thought he was after a sugar mama. Some of his friends were alarmed when debt collectors called him several times a day about the $20,000 she'd run up on his American Express.

By all reports, he truly loved her kids and enjoyed time with them. Even though he hadn't been ready to have babies of his own, he was concerned when she called him from a convenience store phone soon after she miscarried the twins she'd told him she was carrying—redheaded boys like him, she said.

Her spending and debts staggered Alan. They'd simply agreed she would pay the mortgage and he'd take care of the rest of their expenses. He wasn't prepared for her expensive tastes, and he'd never seen proof of her financial resources. Shy of their first anniversary, they split. A friend offered Alan a place to stay.

After one month apart, Sandra called, asking him to help her move some things at their mini-storage unit. At 4:50 p.m. on Saturday evening, as the

December dusk set in, Alan waved goodbye to his friend and left to meet Sandra at the Garland warehouse.

A bit over an hour later, at 6:15 p.m., Sandra called Alan's friend, asking where Alan was. He hadn't shown up. Typical for him, she said, to stand her up. His friend thought it odd—he'd just watched him leave to meet her.

Sandra didn't report Alan missing. He just took off like that sometimes, she said. Finally, on Monday, his work colleagues filed a police report. Two days later, on Wednesday, December 11, 1985, Alan's Ford Bronco was found three and a half hours from Dallas, parked near an electric substation at Southwest Thirty-Sixth and MacArthur, not far from the Oklahoma City Airport.

Oklahoma City police officers found Alan inside, slumped between the front seats. Despite the frigid temperatures, he wore the shorts and T-shirt he'd worn when he waved goodbye on Saturday in Dallas. The autopsy said he had died almost instantly when a .38-caliber round entered his side, piercing his heart. He'd also been shot in the head. Whoever shot him had been sitting in the passenger seat. One report said he had a hamburger and french fries in his stomach, a bite still lodged in his throat, signs he'd been comfortable enough with whoever sat beside him to be eating when he died.

For his burial, Sandra picked out the cheapest casket available and then showed up late to the service, wearing a full mink coat. She spoke with Oklahoma City detectives once and then headed back to Dallas after the funeral, ignoring their request for another interview. Her high-profile lawyer informed the police that neither Sandra nor her children had anything to say to them.

With jurisdictions split between two states, two cities, two hundred miles apart, the investigation faced challenges other than the new widow's silence. While she wasn't talking, other people were, including Alan's mother, Gloria Rehrig, and a tipster dubbed the Highland Park "Deep Throat," after the anonymous informant in the Watergate affair.

As with Betsy Bagwell's death, investigations raise uncomfortable questions and can ferret out inconsistent answers. Sandra had been telling friends and family that Alan was involved in drugs and gambling. She told private investigator Bill Dear and others that she feared for her life.

Bill Dear helped her by checking out the security arrangements around her house but also found enough inconsistencies in Sandra's stories that he bowed out of the case. He found no threats and no evidence of drugs or gambling. What else had she manufactured? Dear was concerned enough to offer to share his file with police, despite cautions from Sandra's defense lawyer, but police investigators reportedly didn't want to give credence to a publicity-magnet PI like Bill Dear.

What might have been discovered had police known what Bill Dear and Dr. Bagwell's private investigator had found—that Sandra had a cellphone, that her stories were inconsistent or that she'd had a hysterectomy years before she told Alan Rehrig she was pregnant and ready to get married? What if they'd been able to compare her alibi with accounts from her children? What if forensics had been advanced enough to track cellphone movement or to more accurately detail time of death?

On the Move

Her children faced increasing ostracism from their friends and Highland Park parents, so Sandra left her dream Dallas neighborhood and moved across the country to a rental house in upscale Marin County, across the bay from San Francisco.

By now, her pattern had become well established. She was a good mother, kept a beautiful house, cooked gourmet meals and was socially and charitably engaged—and she needed a rich husband and wasn't afraid to ask others to help her find him.

As always in the stories that circulated about Sandra, whether she was the demon or the plagued depended on who was telling the story. What surfaced in the reports of her time in California suggested a more deliberate pattern of separating men from their money, by means other than marriage if necessary. At least two men filed suit against her in California, claiming she defrauded them. For those familiar with her story, the web she wove would be new but not surprising. She said her trust fund was tied up and asked if she could borrow money to pay her $3,000-per-month rent—pricey even in Marin County in the 1980s. Could he pay her children's tuition, her car repair bill, her phone bill or her plane ticket to fly east to see her ill daughter? The requests kept coming and got larger; she even asked one man to buy her a Jeep Cherokee. He refused. She hadn't met the deadline they'd set for her to repay what she already owed him.

She told one man, "The second I get it, you'll get it." To another, she said, "I don't owe you this money. I think you gave it to me."

The men she inveigled, the places she lived, the plots she wove, all took on a dizzying, complex pattern, but always with common elements linking them. Police work bounced against jurisdictional boundaries, but the growing reach of the internet, Alan's distraught mother and the diligent work of journalists—in particular Glenna Whitley of the *Dallas Observer* and journalists Eric Miller and Skip Hollandsworth—were able to follow Sandra, salting her path.

The investigative piece by Miller and Hollandsworth, "The Black Widow," appeared in *D Magazine* in May 1987, eighteen months after Alan Rehrig's death. That article may have prompted her departure for California, but then someone anonymously mailed the article to people who knew her in Marin County. The story detailed the deaths of her three husbands—to suicide, cancer and murder—and the suspicious suicide of her friend Betsy Bagwell. One of her California friends was quoted (anonymously) as saying, "Even in weird California, this is too weird to be believed."

Sandra took to moving faster, staying farther beneath the radar, out of news headlines and court filings when possible, in places as dispersed as Boston, Connecticut, Hawaii, Tucson and Atlanta. She also modified her origin story. By the early 2000s, she was in her sixties. The once sexy, seductive, helpless belle was likely less effective at baiting the hook. So, Sandra got religion. In particular, she became an adherent of "prosperity gospel" evangelists who promise that, in exchange for "seed" gifts sent to them, the Lord would send riches and answer dreams specifically for the seed-senders.

According to handwritten notes found among some of her abandoned possessions, Sandra was both a seed-sender and an active seeker after those who would send her money to help her realize her dreams. Her "dream" notes were specific: a multimillion-dollar compound where she could launch her own mission work and a gold Lexus with "Michelin tires" and "custom café au lait seatcovers."

Churches provided a ready supply of people who wanted to help such a charming, mission-minded woman. She still had lustrous dark eyes that focused intently on her audience, and she still knew how to spin a story that spoke to what they wanted to hear. She told of her selfless work in poor countries and her far-flung missionary trips. Her well-told tales invited people to admire her, to feel impelled to help her unless they wanted to fall short of her own shining ideal.

In most cases, she got a place to stay for a while and meals—at one place, expensive organic foods only, by her request—and nice wines or Champagne. The exact map of where she went or an exact tally of those who helped her would be almost impossible to reconstruct.

Left: A pirate flag at a Southport waterfront home, commemorating some of the area's more famous "criminal" visitors. *Photo by Cathy Pickens.*

Right: Southport's waterfront park, with Bald Head Island lighthouse in the distance. *Photo by Cathy Pickens.*

An important turn in her story, though, is easy to identify. In mid-2006, she met Sue Moseley in Southport, North Carolina—through church connections, of course. When she met the former pastor outside the grocery store, she called herself Camille Bowers—her middle name, plus her maiden name Powers morphed a bit, making her harder to track on the internet. The pastor introduced her to Ms. Moseley's sister. Eventually, she moved in with Moseley, just for the few months before her next foreign mission trip. Meanwhile, she would cook and clean at Moseley's beautiful golf community home.

Camille/Sandra asked Ms. Moseley and real estate agent Jack Vereene to help her find a large property suitable for her planned missionary training compound. That $2.7 million house sitting on the intracoastal waterway in Southport would be perfect, she said, and she'd pay cash. But the real estate agent was confused. Why would a missionary need an expensive home in a gated community?

By 2007, Google was able to deliver what Vereene needed, even though he didn't have her correct name. "Missionary" was one search term he entered, along with places she said she'd lived. Glenna Whitley's *Dallas Observer* coverage popped up, with the multipart story and photographs. Vereene called Whitley, who "hadn't heard boo about Sandra/Camille in three years."

Vereene knew Ms. Moseley was safe for the time being; she was staying with her son, Jim, while Sandra traveled on one of her mission trips. When Vereene alerted Jim, he started his own investigation.

While staying with Ms. Moseley, Sandra managed Moseley's mail, answered her phone calls and even set out her medicine for her, leaving water by her bedside, although Ms. Moseley thought that was getting to be a bit intrusive. Jim learned that she'd also diverted the mortgage payments; his mother's house was about to be forced into foreclosure. According to a *Dateline* episode, Sandra charged $2,500 on Moseley's credit cards and forged almost $900 in checks. Someone had also tried to change the information for Moseley's Social Security accounts and the beneficiary on Moseley's life insurance policies.

Jim Moseley pieced together the paper trail and took the information to police, who issued a warrant for Sandra's arrest.

After all he'd learned, Jim Moseley had to be surprised and relieved when Sandra reappeared, calling him to say she was back from her mission trip. She cheerfully announced she was ready to take his mother back to her Southport home near the water.

They arranged to meet at a Dean & Deluca in Charlotte on March 2, 2007. Sandra thought she would pick up the car and take Ms. Moseley back to Southport. Her son arrived with officers from the Violent Criminals Apprehension Team.

Instead of handing her the car keys, Moseley handed her over to the officers, who arrested her. She was held on $1.5 million bond because of her flight risk. Almost one year after her arrest, at age sixty-three, she appeared in federal court in February 2008 to plead guilty to fraud and forgery charges.

Thanks to producers with A&E's *Cold Case Files*, one very interested observer was present in the courtroom: Alan Rehrig's mother, Gloria. They'd flown her from Oklahoma so she could witness Sandra Bridewell enter her guilty plea.

Sandra walked in, only feet away from Glo, as her friends called her. Sandra's hair was gray to shoulder-length, where the faded black dye had grown out during her incarceration. She was handcuffed and shackled, wearing an orange inmate jumpsuit. Sandra held her head high, eyes straight ahead, not acknowledging Gloria or the large button she wore showing

Alan's photo. One of Gloria's friends said Gloria hadn't needed an airplane to fly home to Oklahoma after the hearing, she was so elated.

Although Sandra remains the lone suspect in the death of Alan Rehrig, no charges have been filed. The other deaths that occurred in her orbit remain officially closed. That day in North Carolina, she accepted a plea deal for the fraud and forgery charges: a $250,000 fine, $1,600 in restitution to Sue Moseley and two years in prison. Prosecutors hadn't wanted to risk a trial, concerned she might charm one or more jurors and avoid a conviction. She was, after all, quite charming. And she'd gotten better at disappearing off the radar,

The other witness to that day in court was Glenna Whitley, the reporter who'd dogged the story from Dallas to California to North Carolina. What if that heartbroken mother and that old-school, shoe-leather reporter hadn't kept on the case? What if the news accounts and the magazine article hadn't been there for worried family members to find when the charming, sweet woman asked them for help, for a place to stay, for a donation?

Sandra Camille Powers Stegall Bridewell Rehrig Dandridge served her time and was released. She lived for a time in Marion, North Carolina, but moved on, registering her disapproval of what she found in Marion on her Facebook page, where she identified herself as "works at missionary, I work for the Lord."

UNDETERMINED

When someone dies, officials slot the manner of death into one of five categories: natural causes, accident, suicide or homicide, with "undetermined" reserved for deaths that don't provably fit into one of the other categories.

In North Carolina in 2017, most deaths were natural (diseases and old age fill eight of the top ten causes of death), followed by accident (roughly 6,000 deaths, third-leading cause), suicide (1,500, tenth-leading cause) and homicide (679 deaths). Drug overdose deaths were an alarming 2,400, usually classified as accidental. Equally alarming, suicide was more than twice as common as homicide. Murder stories headline the news almost daily. Suicide, though, is discussed only in respectful whispers. For families, the loss is the same—each is difficult to grieve for its own reasons.

If suicide and homicide are hard to comprehend and grieve, what of that "undetermined" category? How can a family deal with not knowing whether a loved one took her own life? Or with not knowing if a killer is still wandering the streets, perhaps looking for another victim and living life unpunished?

The family of Davina Buff Jones started living with those questions in October 1999 as soon as they learned she'd been found dead near the landmark Bald Head Island Lighthouse with a gunshot wound to the back of her head. Davina was dead. How and why are still unanswered, decades later.

Bald Head Island Lighthouse, the oldest of the North Carolina lighthouses still standing; built in 1817 and almost 110 feet high. *Photo by Cathy Pickens.*

Davina served as an officer with the Bald Head Island Police Department. For a police officer, Davina was tiny—less than five feet tall and less than one hundred pounds. But from her days growing up in Charlotte, the middle of three daughters, attending West Charlotte High School and working at the

Peddler Steakhouse owned by her parents (later site of the Embassy Suites on South Tryon Street), she'd always played bigger than her size.

Her parents retired to the North Carolina coast, to Oak Island. After trying some other jobs, Davina got her law enforcement training—the oldest graduate in her class at age thirty-three. She'd been working for the Bald Head Island department for less than a year, a rookie still learning the subtle judgment calls often needed in policing—when to crack down, when to be stern, when to use humor or issue a warning rather than write a ticket or click the cuffs.

She had her share of rookie run-ins. She had never been one to back down or cut slack when she was responsible for keeping the rules, not even for the island's rich beach house owners or the influx of summer renters.

As North Carolina's southernmost barrier island, Bald Head Island sits between the wide mouth of the Cape Fear River and the Atlantic Ocean, south of Wilmington and only a twenty-minute ferry ride from the waterside town of Southport. On Bald Head, only golf carts or foot travel are allowed—except for police, fire and other service vehicles. Only 20 percent of the island can be developed. The rest is maintained as a nature preserve of marshes and maritime forest. The amenities are quaint: a post office, a few restaurants and bars around the marina, a museum and, of course, the lighthouse. The houses tend to be large, clustered to take advantage of expansive water views that few can afford and many covet. Most staying on the island are part-time residents or tourist renters.

In October 1999, after less than one year with the island department, Davina started applying elsewhere for a new job. She felt she had gotten crosswise with some on the island, both residents and colleagues, especially after she filed a sexual harassment complaint against a local EMS worker. There'd also been complaints about her sometimes abrupt manner with residents.

Davina's boss, Chief Karen Grasty, was supportive, but she'd recently required Davina to patrol only with another officer and not alone. That was akin to a demotion to rookie status, but Grasty pointed out it was for Davina's protection, so she would have a witness if any other residents complained about her. Davina had to wonder what that meant for her future with the department.

In addition, her romantic relationship with an officer from a nearby jurisdiction had recently ended, and he'd moved out of her house. Considering all that had happened, it looked like a good time for new beginnings. After all, she was ambitious and couldn't expect much upward mobility in a small department.

Marsh grass and natural preserve on Bald Head Island. *Photo by Cathy Pickens*.

The Scene

The evening of October 22, 1999, a few days before Halloween, she and her partner, Keith Ray Cane, made their usual ferry commute from Southport to start their twelve-hour night shift at 6:30 p.m. That evening, they patrolled as usual in separate trucks, he driving a Chevy Blazer and she driving a Ford Ranger pickup truck—her feet could best reach the pedals in that truck.

They took their usual 10:00 p.m. dinner break, which was interrupted by a call about a missing golf cart at the marina's River Pilot Café. No one was around when they drove over to answer the call. However, they'd earlier spotted a golf cart near the lighthouse, so they rode over, found it and recorded the registration number to check ownership.

Returning to the station, Officer Cane went back to his unfinished dinner. Davina checked something on the computer, although the later investigation didn't record what she'd searched for or found. She then left, saying she was going to ride around. She didn't give any details. That had been their routine before she'd been told not to ride alone.

She went to the marina pay phone—a red call box where visitors invariably stop for photos—to call her now ex-boyfriend at 11:19 p.m. They talked only for a few minutes. He later said she'd called to make sure they were still friends. He told investigators he'd assured her they were. She then patrolled toward the lighthouse.

Old Baldy, as it's called, is the oldest of the seven remaining lighthouses along the North Carolina coast. Unlike the towering black-and-white spiral-striped Cape Hatteras lighthouse, Old Baldy isn't the most picturesque. It looks like something kids built with buckets of wet gray-brown sand. But it has its own stubby charm, and its light still shines, though pointed up into the night sky and no longer sweeping the coast as a navigational guide. The area around it was sparsely lit. A cart path ran near the lighthouse. The town offices, visitor's center and post office stood nearby.

That night, Davina's next documented activity was her call to dispatch at 11:48 p.m.: "C-COM, 4206. Show me out with three. Stand by, stand by, please." Her badge number was 4206. In cop talk, she had stopped or approached three individuals. She was asking the dispatcher to keep the line open. Her next words recorded over the microphone were clear and deliberate, delivered in a measured cop voice: "There ain't no reason to have a gun here on Bald Head Island, OK? You wanna put down the gun. Come on, do us a favor and put down—"

Left: Ferry docked at Bald Head Island in 2019. *Photo by Cathy Pickens.*

Right: Entry door to Bald Head Island Lighthouse. *Photo by Cathy Pickens.*

The next sounds were electronic crackling or feedback squeals. Her partner, Officer Cane, heard the transmissions in the police station. He headed out the door and straight for his Blazer to look for her as soon as she said, "Show me out with three." He couldn't find her or anyone else. Then he saw parking lights by the lighthouse, in a cul-de-sac. A path from that little-used cul-de-sac connected with the marina road and the boat dock; a navigable creek ran nearby.

He found her truck, lights on, motor running, backed into the cul-de-sac and facing the lighthouse. One thing he knew about Davina was that she always followed procedure and carried her heavy flashlight with her when she got out of the truck at night. Not this time. He saw it lying on the truck seat.

He found her, lying facedown on the road behind her truck. He felt no pulse. Her service gun—a .40-caliber Glock semiautomatic—was out of the holster and on the ground, her right hand resting on it.

Kent Brown, the fire and EMS chief, responded to Officer Cane's backup call. Worried that a shooter might still be in the area, the first responders treated the scene as a "hot" zone. When the paramedics arrived, they

Quiet road to the lighthouse and Bald Head Island Town Hall and Post Office. *Photo by Cathy Pickens.*

Left: Golf cart parking near lighthouse and museum, near where the truck was found. *Photo by Cathy Pickens*.

Right: Fence near where the body was found, beside the lighthouse. *Photo by Cathy Pickens*.

retrieved her as if from a battlefield, grabbing her by her service belt and a leg (or shoulder, accounts differ) and carrying her to a safer location. What happened next continued to be debated decades later.

The Aftermath

Chief Karen Grasty was on disability leave but headed to the island as soon as she was alerted. By the time she got there, the body had been moved dockside, sitting on an uncovered gurney. Grasty had it taken inside the ferry office; she noted the hands had not been bagged to preserve any evidence under the fingernails.

This was a small island without crime scene investigators on site. This occurred the year before the *CSI* franchise hit television and introduced viewers to the details of crime scene preservation, the bagging of hands, the knowledge that tiny bits of evidence could solve a crime—at least in the roughly forty-two minutes it takes each episode to air.

In real life, on a dark October night at a secluded and usually tranquil spot, people faced with the unthinkable may not always make the best decisions. After all, who would expect a police officer to be killed in the line of duty on a wealthy little vacation island?

Chief Grasty left orders that what remained of the crime scene be protected while she crossed to the mainland to handle questions from the press. When she returned, she found the area no longer surrounded by crime scene tape. The fire department had been asked to hose the blood from the scene, reportedly because a wedding and photos were scheduled for that weekend. The source of that request was never confirmed.

Blood spatter and drag marks observed by some on scene that night, along with any other evidence, were gone. Officers hadn't been able to search the scene adequately in the dark, and the scene had not been properly photographed. As an example, a shell casing near the picket fence was shown lying in one orientation in one photo, sitting at another angle in a second photo. Very little of the scene was preserved or recorded.

From the first, this wasn't a textbook or made-for-television investigation, in part because Bald Head Island isn't a well-equipped metropolitan area with highly trained professionals and state-of-the-art equipment quickly available. Accessible only by water, Bald Head is an island near a series of small municipalities. While small-town life has its advantages, quick access to tools and support found in big cities isn't one of them.

As with most investigations into a sudden death, each piece of evidence slots into columns, pointing to one manner of death or another. In this case, each element uncovered fell into either the "suicide" or "homicide" column. Both columns had plenty of entries.

The initial medical examination was rushed because the doctor wanted to get the information to the investigators in the field as quickly as possible. But the rush meant mistakes and maybe headed the investigation down a wrong path. For starters, the doctor sketched the bullet wound closer to the right ear than to the center of the back of her head. Later autopsy photos show the exact location of the wound, leaving no doubt, but as first described, the wound looked like one that could've easily been self-inflicted. That initial assessment led the early investigators toward the conclusion that she'd shot herself, an assumption that seemed to set the direction from the beginning.

State Bureau of Investigation (SBI) agents were called in and took the lead, along with the Brunswick County Sheriff's Office. Officers from area jurisdictions and from the Highway Patrol were also involved. Officers searched Davina's house and found her two beloved Australian shepherds. She'd recently built a covered run for them so they could get outside during her long workdays. They found her journals and the notes she routinely scribbled on used envelopes and scraps of paper. They found her to-do list for the following day, which included getting heartworm pills for her dogs, her own prescription and an oil change and new shocks for her truck. She wrote everything about her life on those old envelopes and scraps of paper and notebooks. She always kept journals, filled with details. Nothing in her writing indicated a plan for ending her life.

Davina had seen her family doctor recently and switched to a new antidepressant. Years earlier, as a teen, Davina had made suicidal gestures. She sometimes talked about "if I'm not here." She recently told her doctor that she'd thought about just swimming out into the ocean. They talked that over; her doctor made her promise to contact him immediately if she ever felt she might act on her thoughts. He assessed her as only a "low risk" of suicide.

On the day of her death, people described her as upbeat. That can signal that a suicidal person has come to a decision. The buoyant attitude says, "Soon, I'll be over all this." But those who saw her also said in the same breath, "Nothing was different." She was usually upbeat, loud, talkative and energetic. She was herself on that last day.

Her family and friends pointed out she'd had two broken marriages before she turned thirty and that other relationships had ended. She'd survived those without derailing. She read romance novels and believed in happy-ever-afters. She passionately loved her dogs and wouldn't abandon them without making sure they were cared for.

Her mental health history certainly influenced the investigation. Sure, she was on antidepressants and seeing doctors regularly, but those who knew her said that was evidence she was self-aware and taking the right steps to care for herself.

Tiny Bald Head Island might not seem to hold much promise or excitement for an officer who loved investigations and wanted to work undercover in a bigger jurisdiction. But the lighthouse sits near a creek that smugglers used over several centuries. Davina had recently spoken to her father and at least one other law enforcement officer about drug smuggling in the area. As eighteenth-century pirates had learned, the tidewater creeks and inlets made for easy drop-off points and hidey-holes. Reports hinted that the U.S. Drug Enforcement Agency had investigated at least one drug drop-off in the area, although that had been years earlier.

In part because the initial crime scene was destroyed, in part because of limited resources available on the island that night and in part because of the challenges of an unwitnessed act, nothing about the investigation satisfied anyone who wanted it resolved.

The regional medical examiner in Jacksonville, North Carolina, with more experience with violent death than the local doctor who did the quick initial exam, tracked the bullet trajectory as slightly upward and to the left. With the contact wound to the back of her head (suicides rarely hold the gun away from their bodies), he concluded that suicide was "highly possible."

Despite the early hints of suicide, possible murder suspects were also investigated. The night of her death, three men tried to sneak aboard the ferry. The accounts of the case don't adequately explain how they hoped to escape notice or how they were cleared of involvement, but law enforcement didn't consider them a viable lead. Were they landscape workers seen on the island earlier? Were they island regulars who may have been drunk but not involved? Was it just a coincidence Davina's last radio transmission said she was "out with three"?

After considering the evidence, Brunswick County district attorney Rex Gore concluded that the officer's death was a suicide. The case required no further investigation.

Davina's family was stunned. They suspected an attempt to hush things quickly, to avoid bad publicity for the tourist-dependent area. The family marshaled their resolve and set about forcing the state to do more than what they saw as a cursory dismissal of Davina's life, a coverup of a crime.

The family filed civil proceedings with the federal Justice Department and the state Industrial Commission because, they contended, she had been killed on the job. Workers killed on the job are entitled to compensation, with special consideration for law enforcement officers; suicides receive no compensation. Her family's passion for clearing her name, not money, was the force that drove them.

In 2007, Elaine Buff (a pen name) self-published her account of the case, *Out with Three*, full of interviews, official documents, autopsy and crime scene drawings and photos, along with the family's unanswered questions.

While speculation circled around Davina's mental condition, the key question was mechanical: could she have held her service Glock behind her head and pulled the trigger to create the bullet trajectory that killed her?

In various settings and hearings, women of different sizes tested it. If she had held the gun in both hands and aimed it at her face, with her thumb on the trigger, then lifted her hands over and behind her head, holding the gun upside down, maybe she could get the muzzle in place. She was smaller than most women. Even if she could exert the required force with her thumb, getting the slightly upward trajectory complicated the maneuver even further. Possible…but likely? When others mimicked the move, the trajectory tended to be downward, rather than upward and to the left. In addition, if she held the Glock upside down—the most likely posture—the shell casing ejected to the left; the shell casing was found to the right of her body. Her family continued to spend money and energy to make sure truth, not just convenience, was pursued.

In 2005, the North Carolina Industrial Commission held hearings where attorneys representing both the State of North Carolina and the family asked questions and presented evidence. Interested parties lined up on either side of the murder/suicide question. Experts cited studies showing that a shot to the back of the head is "very rare in general" and, when it occurs, is overwhelmingly more common in cases of homicide than in suicide.

Some town officials and then police chief Karen Grasty believed Davina was murdered, that the investigation let her down. Others believed that a suicide ruling benefited the residents and land developers; murder might be bad for property values and tourism. It'd be best if ended quickly, with no memorials of a slain officer. No one wants a vacation paradise with a killer wandering loose, one willing to kill a police officer. That's just bad for business.

Attorneys for Davina's family hired an expert in suicidology. His psychological autopsy on Davina found no evidence of motive or the impulsivity usually seen with suicide.

The Industrial Commission held that "the greater weight of the evidence" did not show she was suicidal at the time of her death, that it was "highly unlikely" she could have held the pistol "to achieve the trajectory" and that she was "a law enforcement officer killed in the line of duty." Her estate received $50,000 and an additional $12,500 in attorney's fees. The U.S. Department of Justice later awarded $147,000 from the federal Public Safety Officers' Benefits Office. Those decisions provided some vindication in the family's fight to speak for Davina, although no suspect was identified or prosecuted.

In 2005, local district attorney Rex Gore asked the SBI to give the case a fresh look. After a year, the review criticized some of the Industrial Commission's assumptions, and based on her mental state, the SBI's report decided that her death looked more like a staged suicide.

Unpaved path on Bald Head Island. *Photo by Cathy Pickens.*

In 2010, a new district attorney, Jon David, took office and pledged to again look at the case. Davina's family had been tireless in pushing for answers to the questions still festering about that night. Without their efforts, the case would evaporated from most folks' ken, living only in "did you know…" whispers.

District Attorney David pulled together a blue-ribbon panel of five former Federal Bureau of Investigation agents with years of experience, various specializations, no prior involvement with the case and no loyalties. They went back over the entire case, revisited the detailed Industrial Commission findings but, of course, couldn't reconstruct a crime scene that hadn't been properly documented. Their investigation ended where it was probably destined to end: unresolved. The expert investigators were split on the question of homicide or suicide.

But the family won a concession. On December 12, 2017, the district attorney announced that the review concurred with the Industrial Commission's determination that "serious questions existed concerning the suicide." The official determination was changed from "suicide" to "undetermined."

Of the five official categories of death, not one can bring back a loved one. While "undetermined" has to be the most unsatisfying resolution, the one that leaves the wound unhealed, it also kept this case officially "open."

In the leafy green shadows at the base of Old Baldy, with the waving seagrass and parades of golf carts and bicycles enjoying the slow pace of an idyllic island, the question of what happened to Officer Davina Buff Jones on that October night in 1999 seems undetermined and unanswerable.

THE MISSING AND THE MISSED

Currituck County

Little Kenneth Beasley

In a world with the faces of missing children on milk cartons and on bulletin boards inside every Walmart, a world where tales of kidnapped children *aren't* broadcast is hard to imagine.

Visiting the Outer Banks and the tidewater regions, it's also hard to imagine just how rural the area would have been more than one hundred years ago. No weather-beaten cottages or soaring multi-bedroom beach houses clustering against the oceanfront dunes. No recreational fishing piers jutting into the surf or vacationing families. No suburbs spilling over from growing urban areas into what had been fishing villages and farmland and family holdings. No four-lane blacktops speeding traffic into the upper reaches of Currituck County, the state's northernmost stretch of barrier islands and sounds.

It's easy to see how those living along the neighboring swamps and rivers would know if a local state senator's little boy went missing. The news would surely reach as far as Raleigh, where his father served in the state legislature. What's hard to imagine is how such a story would fizzle into only short news reports by the time it reached Charlotte or Norfolk. The *Statesville Landmark* reported, on page three, that the senator's son had "mysteriously disappeared Monday and at last account no trace of him had been found."

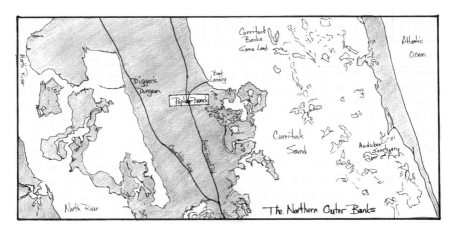

Aerial of Poplar Branch, surrounded by dense forest and water. The school sits on Highway 136 past the fork; Beasley's boat landing is at road's end. *Map by Cathy Pickens.*

When a child goes missing now, Amber alerts, news broadcasts and social media carry the message, far and quick. Of course, even with alerts broadcast by internet and constant television news, no family thinks the message goes far enough or fast enough. No parent is satisfied that officials are as frantic or as diligent or as dedicated as they want them to be. It's *their* child who is missing, and no one can care more than they do.

But imagine Valentine's Day 1905, in rural tidewater Currituck County, in the far reaches of the coast closer to Norfolk, Virginia, than to any densely settled part of North Carolina, when a specially chartered train was needed to carry Senator Samuel M. Beasley on the last leg of his journey home after he received a telegram bearing the troubling news.

The day before the train left Raleigh to take him cross-state, his eight-year-old son, Kenneth, went missing from school. No instant news or interstates, only slow-motion panic, frustration and fear.

Kenneth Beasley was the middle child between older brother Moran, age seventeen, and little sister Ethel, age four. Moran attended school in Elizabeth City. Ethel, of course, was too young for school and stayed home with their mother. Kenneth could walk to his school. He only had to bear right onto the road that headed out to the boat landing his father owned, a little over a half-mile walk from home to school.

His small school was held at the Odd Fellows Hall, which now serves as a private residence, just one city block's distance down the road from the current Poplar Branch Post Office.

Above: Train tracks through dense forest. *Courtesy of Antoine Beauvillain on Unsplash.*

Left: Fork on Highway 136 viewed from the current Poplar Branch Post Office. *Photo by Cathy Pickens.*

Left: Former Odd Fellows Hall and Kenneth Beasley's school, now a private residence, viewed from current Poplar Branch Post Office. *Photo by Cathy Pickens.*

Right: View of former school from the crossroads. The school is the last house on the left of the road; the post office roof is visible on the right. *Photo by Cathy Pickens.*

The Beasleys lived in the Poplar Branch community, with a gathering of houses, the post office and Wilson Woodhouse's store—about fifty miles from Norfolk and thirty miles from Elizabeth City. Samuel Beasley, a farmer, had opened the Poplar Branch boat landing only a few years before, for commercial fishing and transport rather than for the pleasure boats that use the landing now.

February that year was cold and brought snow—a rarity for the coast. Winter weather near the water can bring a damp, chilling cold. Kenneth bundled up in his suit, cap, coat and gloves that morning, announcing to his mother on the way out the door, "I've seen some mighty pretty puppies and I want one."

The school had two teachers: Miss Nina Harrison, who taught the four lower grades, including Kenneth's third-grade level, and Professor M.P. Jennings, who taught the older students and served as head of the school.

Despite the cold, the rain and snow cleared in time for the noon recess. Anyone who has been eight years old knows how exciting that time of pale winter sun and escape would have been. His friends said that Kenneth

Former site of Samuel Beasley's Poplar Branch commercial boat landing on Currituck Sound, now a public boat access. *Photo by Cathy Pickens.*

Dense undergrowth typical of the area, behind the current Poplar Branch Post Office across from the old school. *Photo by Cathy Pickens*.

played outside during recess, but when the afternoon bell rang at 1:00 p.m., Kenneth told his cousin Benny Walker, "I'm going farther back," and disappeared into the woods.

Neither his cousin nor any of the other students could or would say what drew Kenneth into the woods just at the time he was supposed to be going back to class. Did it have anything to do with those puppies? Either he didn't plan to stay gone long, or in the way of young boys, he didn't think about it getting colder; he left his coat and gloves hanging inside the school building.

Miss Nina reported his absence to Professor Jennings, who sent a boy to search and then sent Kenneth's cousin for a more thorough look. When cousin Benny wound up at the Woodhouse store about an hour after Kenneth left, the storekeeper knew they needed more than just one boy searching.

Woodhouse prompted the professor to send out the older boys while he alerted the neighbors. Many of them regularly hunted in those woods and wetlands. They knew the hidden animal trails and how to navigate, but that didn't make the woods and undergrowth any less dense.

The rain returned, then the snow. Despite a search into the night and again the next day, with as many as three hundred men volunteering, they found no sign of Kenneth.

The day after his son disappeared, Valentine's Day, Senator Beasley received the heartbreaking telegram in Raleigh. By train and horse-drawn carriage, he arrived home in Poplar Branch at midnight, hoping that he'd see his son safe when he got there.

The mystery only deepened. Hunters knew the dangers of those woods and swamps, but presumably so did Kenneth. An energetic kid who had grown up playing along those creeks and marshes would know the pattern of flooding and dry land, as well as the fish, snakes, lizards and birds; he would know how to navigate the area as well or better than the grown-ups.

The searchers went calling on the only reported "resident" of the woods around Maple Swamp: a man in a distant cabin, identified as a "foreigner" or a "Yankee." Someone said they'd heard a child's cry for help coming from that vicinity. But the mystery man had decamped long before, and they found no sign of Kenneth.

Other rumors began to circulate. The most publicized came almost two weeks after Kenneth disappeared, in a letter reportedly written to "a gentleman of Raleigh" from "a resident of Currituck County," printed in the *Raleigh News & Observer* on February 24 and reprinted in Manly Wade Wellman's 1954 account of the case:

The Senator's Son, Charles Oldham's investigation into the Beasley case. *Courtesy of Beach Glass Books.*

There was a strange man seen up about Barco postoffice and two more places by three different men. He was in a buggy drawn by a black mule and had the boy down between his knees, but the people saw him before they heard that the boy was missing. These men that saw him say that the boy was crying and seemed dissatisfied, but the man was talking to him rough.

For his well-researched 2018 account of the case, *The Senator's Son*, attorney and author Charles Oldham dug into the mostly handwritten historic and legal records to capture the political backdrop and long-buried details. Oldham found that neither the letter writer nor the recipient was ever identified. Maybe the letter didn't exist but was created only to document the rumors. But others also reported seeing a boy in a buggy in the Barco area, about ten miles north of Poplar Branch on Highway 158 on the way to Norfolk.

After this published letter, further searching of the swamp or watching the water for a body to float to the surface became futile. Kenneth Beasley had apparently been kidnapped. But why? And by whom? Where was he now? Why had there been no ransom request?

History of Child Kidnapping

Today, names like Jaycee Dugard (kidnapped when she was eleven and held by a man and his wife in their Northern California backyard for eighteen years) and Elizabeth Smart (taken from her Utah home by a handyman who'd done work at her parents' home and held by the "prophet" and his wife for nine months) are well known. Few people realize how very rare kidnappings by strangers are—and always have been.

When little Charley Ross was kidnapped in 1874, his was the first highly publicized *cause célèbre* child kidnapping in the country. His parents were prominent in Philadelphia but not nearly as wealthy as the kidnappers thought when they demanded $20,000 in ransom, worth close to $500,000 in 2020.

Laws are written to respond to wrongdoing, not to anticipate it. At the time that four-year-old Charley Ross and his five-year-old brother, Walter, were lured into a horse-drawn carriage with the promise of firecrackers, kidnapping wasn't a specific criminal offense in Pennsylvania. Kidnapping was such an oddity that most states had no laws against it.

Little Walter ran into a store to buy fireworks with the money the men gave him. The carriage left without him, carrying off Charley.

Charley's family soon began receiving ransom notes. Charley's father, Christian, faced not just the absence of laws but also the absence of a playbook for dealing with kidnappers. The common wisdom was "don't deal with kidnappers." Officials warned him that, if he did, he might make it open season on any children whose parents appeared able to pay a ransom. The ensuing "should we or shouldn't we" wrangling raised an ethical dilemma that ignited debate beyond Philadelphia. During the debate, Charley remained missing.

In a surprising development five months later, in Brooklyn, New York, two men were shot while burgling a house. One died immediately. The other lived long enough to say he was sorry and confess to Charley Ross's kidnapping in Philadelphia. In confusing accounts, he said either that Charley was dead or that he would be home soon with his parents.

Charley was never seen again. His parents continued to search for him. Without news media and online resources to get the word out, Charley's father published a book, *The Father's Story of Charley Ross, the Kidnapped Child*, and did speaking engagements to raise money and awareness.

North Carolina state law still didn't cover kidnappings thirty years later, when Kenneth Beasley disappeared in 1905 and was assumed stolen. Even

ABDUCTION OF CHARLIE BREWSTER ROSS.

On July 1st, 1874, at about four o'clock, P. M., Charlie Brewster, and Walter, the latter about six years old, sons of Christian K. Ross, were taken from the side-walk in front of their father's residence, on Washington Lane, Germantown, Pa., by two men in a buggy. Walter was carried about five miles, and there left upon the street; but of Charlie no subsequent clue has been obtained; it is earnestly solicited that every one, who shall receive this circular, make diligent inquiry, and promptly furnish any information obtained, and if the child be found, cause the detention of the parties having him in custody.

This circular must not be posted up, and care must be exercised, that suspicious persons do not obtain access to it.

Members of the press are specially requested to refrain from publishing the interrogatories hereafter given, so that the parties having the child in custody may not obtain the means of training him regarding his answers thereto.

On the discovery of any child, who shall be suspected of being the lost one, a photograph should be immediately obtained, if possible, and forwarded; and photographs of the parents will be sent for identification by the child.

$20,000 REWARD has been offered for the recovery of the child, and conviction of the kidnappers; all claims to which, however, will be relinquished in favor of the parties giving the information which shall lead to this result.

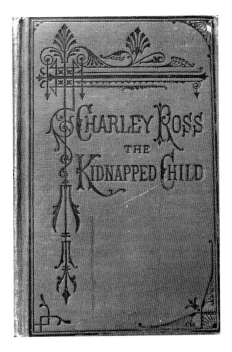

Opposite: Broadside issued by Pinkerton's National Detective Agency offering reward for Charley Ross in 1874, reprinted in the boy's father's book about the case. *Courtesy of Library of Congress*.

Left: The book Charley Ross's father wrote to keep his missing son's story in the public eye. *Photo by Cathy Pickens*.

though many assumed he'd been carried across the nearby state line into Virginia, no federal laws existed to make that transport a crime. Change wouldn't come until almost another thirty years passed.

In the 1930s, gangsters lost income when liquor could once again be bought legally and banks got harder to rob, so some turned to kidnapping rich people in order to relieve them of some wealth—Robin Hoods whose only poor beneficiaries were themselves. Throughout the '30s, gangster kidnappings typically involved holding wealthy business executives for ransom.

At that time, most criminal law was defined by state law. The federal government had relatively few criminal laws. John Dillinger, Ma Barker and her gang, Machine Gun Kelly and Bonnie and Clyde Parker, among others with folk hero status, helped change that.

Anyone who has watched old crime fighting movies or television knows it is illegal to "transport across state lines for immoral purposes." Those invisible state lines are important because, under the U.S. Constitution, states are responsible for the welfare of their citizens and write their own criminal laws. The federal government is involved only in matters involving "interstate commerce." It took a while to legally recognize crime as an enterprise, one that clearly crossed state lines.

Everything changed in 1932 with the brazen kidnapping of the son of a national hero. When aviator Charles Lindbergh's baby was carried down a ladder from his second-floor nursery at the Lindberghs' New Jersey estate, the case became a national cause and national tragedy. The Lindberghs paid a $50,000 ransom, but the child was found dead a few months after he was taken, partially buried not far from their home. Bruno Hauptmann, convicted and later executed, never admitted to the crime, but when asked how it might have happened, he said the child might have fallen when he was carried down the ladder and died that night.

By 1931, states had passed anti-kidnapping laws. Until 1932, though, federal law prohibited only kidnapping for slavery and didn't address the almost three hundred kidnappings reported in 1931.

The Lindbergh kidnapping prompted passage in 1932 of the Lindbergh Law, making kidnapping for ransom and transportation across state lines a federal crime. A victim missing for at least twenty-four hours is presumed to have crossed state lines, activating the FBI's federal "interstate commerce" jurisdiction.

By the early twenty-first century, most child kidnappings were committed by family members or noncustodial parents, a product of the changing nature of families in the last hundred years. Although children are also taken for sexual exploitation, and some are taken by women who want a child to raise, currently fewer than 1 percent of child kidnappings are stranger abductions. All these cases are highly publicized, compared to what was possible when Charley Ross and Kenneth Beasley disappeared. Kidnapping for ransom—of children or adults—is still remarkably rare. For one reason or another, keeping a person alive and hidden for a period of time is tricky, then and now.

The Frontrunner Suspect

Amid searches that failed to find Kenneth Beasley, the disappearance of the strange man in the cabin and stories circulating about the boy in the carriage, the locals, almost from the beginning, had their eye on one of their own: Joshua Harrison.

Joshua Harrison had married well when he married into the Jarvis family; his father-in-law was a respected Methodist minister. His brother-in-law was destined to be the Speaker of the North Carolina House of Commons (elected

Speaker only three years after he first went to Raleigh), a U.S. congressman and the education advocate who helped create East Carolina University.

The anonymous letter printed by the *Raleigh News & Observer* eleven days after Kenneth's disappearance mentioned only one questionable name: "Mr. Joshua Harrison went off Tuesday morning and never got back until Sunday. He claimed he had been in Pasquotank." As author Charles Oldham pointed out, several papers, in reprinting the letter, omitted Harrison's role, maybe to avoid liability for defamation of character.

People in Poplar Branch knew Joshua Harrison. He was a farmer, married into the influential Jarvis family and was the father of Kenneth Beasley's teacher, Miss Nina Harrison. According to Senator Beasley's trial testimony, reported in Oldham's book, he was also "a purveyor of scuppernong wine, as well as a Republican, a scalawag, a terrorizer of the community, and an all-round brute."

Harrison sold liquor without a license—another way of saying he was a bootlegger. But that was only one of the activities that set him on society's margin despite his family connections. In 1865, he had been charged with shooting Caleb Owens in the forehead, killing him instantly. A news account said the gun discharged accidentally. The court report said only that Harrison was found not guilty. In some reports, the victim was black and was working for Harrison. According to the census, he was probably white and about eight years old when he died, the same age as Kenneth Beasley.

Harrison was back in court three years later on a delayed charge for killing an old man five years earlier. Charles Oldham found news reports, dated long after the incident, that supplied a few details. At first, the shooting was treated as an accident. Later, someone came forward saying the victim had blood on the back of his head, claiming it was from a bullet wound. Again, the written record is scant, but news reports say the old man was Harrison's father. Again, the jury found Harrison not guilty.

What really happened? Why the delay in bringing the cases? Was Harrison a popular man, with his liquor and business interests? Or a powerful one? Were people afraid of him? The historical record doesn't make that clear.

What was documented was that Samuel Beasley, to serve his constituents, introduced legislation to limit the sale of liquor. The 1903 bill had a poetic title: "An Act to Prohibit the Manufacture and Sale of Liquors, Cider, or Medicated Bitters Near Certain Churches in Currituck County." While it came as part of a statewide debate over who controlled distilleries, this legislation was unabashedly directed at Harrison's operation as a "purveyor of scuppernong wine" and "terrorizer of the community."

An abandoned Jarvisburg house, south of Poplar Branch. *Courtesy of Carol M. Highsmith's America Project in the Carol M. Highsmith Archive, Library of Congress, Prints and Photographs Division.*

So, naturally, when Kenneth Beasley disappeared almost two years after the Currituck anti-liquor bill first started hampering Harrison's Maple Swamp liquor business, community rumor turned on Harrison. Just because something is rumor doesn't mean it's not at least partly true.

Eighteen months after Kenneth's disappearance, Joshua Harrison was indicted. Arguments over whether the trial should be moved were settled with a change of venue to Elizabeth City and its Pasquotank County Courthouse, a drive that didn't deter Currituck County court-watchers from attending. The trial was, after all, a big deal: nine lawyers seated on both sides, elected officials on both sides—including former governor Jarvis, the defendant's brother-in-law.

The jury deliberated several hours before declaring Harrison guilty. The Raleigh *News & Observer* quoted the tall, slender old man's plea to the sheriff's deputy who escorted him from the courtroom:

> *My God, isn't this awful? I do not know anything about that boy. If they were to take each member of my family, as dearly as I love them, and chowder them before my eyes, I could not tell them any more than I have already told.*

Did it make sense that this bootlegger and scalawag would exact revenge on his nemesis by stealing his son? Was the boy killed? Was he spirited away to Harrison's daughter's boardinghouse in Norfolk, as some suspected? Or did someone else kidnap or kill the boy? Maybe the mysterious man who lived for a time in the swamp house? Or, a true tragedy for everyone concerned, did Kenneth wander away without his coat, get disoriented in the cold, dark swamp and die, never to be found?

Harrison was released pending an appeal, but the post-conviction legal maneuvers failed to win him a new trial or exonerate him. When an officer came to the Norfolk Hotel to take Harrison into custody, Harrison shot and killed himself in his room. He left behind a written statement, his final declaration of innocence.

The case was little reported outside North Carolina and would be little known today except for the legal detective work of attorney and historian Charles Oldham. It remains a case full of sad questions.

Another Missing Boy

The case of yet another missing North Carolina boy received more recent coverage in part because he was found—or was he? Modern DNA technology has provided one answer and opened a lot of questions in the 1912 case of Bobby Dunbar.

North Carolina's role in the case was an odd happenstance. One August morning in 1912, in swamps and bayous as steamy as Louisiana would be that time of year, a group of family and friends went camping and fishing at Swayze's Lake near Opelousas. When everyone gathered for lunch, four-year-old Bobby Dunbar was missing.

Just as with Kenneth Beasley, folks started searching the swampy area. When they found a set of bare footprints walking toward a railroad trestle leading out of the swamps, they feared he'd been taken. A stranger had been seen in the area. They'd already searched the waterways, with no sign of his straw hat (which arguably would have floated) or of his body (which also would have floated, especially after they threw sticks of dynamite into the water to force his body to surface). They hunted and cut open alligators to make sure he hadn't been eaten.

The Dunbars, a well-to-do family from Opelousas, mounted a wide-ranging search for Bobby, sending postcards with a photo and description to towns from Texas to Florida: "Large round blue eyes, hair light, but turning dark, complexion very fair with rosy cheeks, well developed, stout but not very fat. Big toe on left foot badly scarred from burn when a baby."

In April 1913, eight months after Bobby Dunbar disappeared in the swamp, officials in Hub, Mississippi, nabbed William Cantwell Walters and sent a telegram to the Dunbars.

Law enforcement in Hub believed they'd found the missing boy traveling with this itinerant piano tuner from Barnesville, North Carolina, south of Lumberton. No, William Cantwell Walters said, the boy certainly wasn't Bobby Dunbar. He was Bruce Anderson, the illegitimate son of Walters's brother and Julia Anderson, who worked for the Walters family back in North Carolina; the boy was just traveling with him for a while.

Walters was desperate for someone to corroborate his story. After all, by that time, kidnapping in Louisiana was a capital offense, and conviction could mean a death sentence. Julia Anderson claimed he'd taken her child without permission. Maybe he borrowed her son for a bit too long; she apparently didn't much miss him. But kidnapping a stranger? No way, Walters said. This was his nephew, Bruce.

The Dunbars wasted no time getting to Mississippi. Was this Bobby? Even though he hadn't been gone very long, they didn't think he looked much like their little boy. Four-year-olds can change a lot in a short time, but Bobby didn't recognize the Dunbars either.

A Louisiana newspaper paid for Julia Anderson to travel from North Carolina to see if she could identify the son she hadn't seen for fifteen months. After the time he spent with the Dunbars, where he got gifts of a bicycle and a pony and a ride in a fire engine decorated with flowers, the little boy didn't recognize Julia Anderson.

The jury convicted Walters, who served two years in prison before being granted a new trial. The prosecutor decided not to try him a second time, and Walters disappeared from the public record.

Julia Anderson continued to assert that the boy now called Bobby was hers. She moved from North Carolina, settled in Mississippi and raised eight other children, who grew up understanding they had a brother who'd been taken by a family in Louisiana. "Bobby" was raised by the Dunbars.

In both families, the story became part of their family lore. In 1999, Bobby Dunbar's granddaughter received a family scrapbook from her father. Growing up in Winston-Salem, Margaret Cutright had heard about the kidnapping and her grandfather's return home. Now, flipping pages

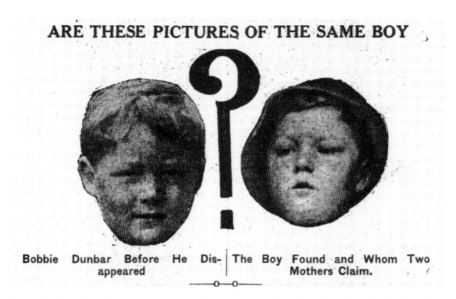

ARE THESE PICTURES OF THE SAME BOY

Bobbie Dunbar Before He Disappeared | The Boy Found and Whom Two Mothers Claim.

From 1914 national newspapers: "Are These Pictures of the Same Boy? (*left*) Bobby Dunbar before he disappeared (*right*) The boy found and whom two mothers claim." *Courtesy Wikimedia Commons*.

and seeing the case unfold in news clippings prompted her to dig into the case. Her detective work led her to the daughter of suspected kidnapper Walters's defense attorney, who still had the nine-hundred-page defense file. In all those typed pages, news reports and editorial cartoons, Cutright started wondering about the links between piney woods North Carolina and a Louisiana swamp and a wealthy family and a woman who didn't have much but children.

Cutright decided to find out if her grandfather was really Bobby Dunbar… or Bruce Anderson. By odd coincidence, Bobby Dunbar's son, Robert, had settled in Kinston, North Carolina, a few hours from where the Walters family still lives in Robeson County and where Julia Anderson lived before she moved to Mississippi.

The 2004 DNA results proved that Cutright's family was not related to the Dunbars. Her grandfather wasn't Bobby Dunbar. William Cantwell Walters told the truth all those years ago—the boy was most likely his illegitimate nephew Bruce, just as he'd said.

According to AP reporter Allen Breed, when Bobby Dunbar Jr.—Cutright's father and the missing boy's namesake—was a teenager, he asked his dad, "How do you know you're Bobby Dunbar?" His dad replied, "I know who I am, and I know who you are. And nothing else makes a difference."

If Bruce Anderson lived his life as Bobby Dunbar, then the question about the real Bobby Dunbar on that Louisiana fishing outing near swampy Swayze's Lake is the same as the question about Kenneth Beasley's disappearance after lunch recess in Poplar Branch: What happened?

BLACK WIDOW II

Lenoir and Jones Counties

Police calls in small towns and rural communities tend to be routine. But a well-known businessman reported missing would be outside the routine. Finding the man lying in the middle of the road would cause concern. Seeing two shotgun wounds to his torso would change everything.

After January 21, 1992, things wouldn't be routine in Kinston for some time to come. The investigation would uncover carefully hidden secrets, upending what folks thought they knew about their neighbors.

Billy White, a Kinston native, owned a successful insurance agency and stayed active in political and civic groups. People in town knew him as friendly and open, always kind. Billy had faced challenges. His first wife, the mother of his three children, became intractably mentally ill and had to be institutionalized. But Sylvia Ipock, the nice widow lady who kept an immaculate house and lived down the street with three sons of her own, had helped when she could as he assumed full responsibility for his household. When he finally made the difficult decision to divorce, it seemed natural that he and Sylvia would marry and combine their households and children in a bigger house on Hodges Road.

When Sylvia told Billy that a new client had called, needing insurance but too busy to come into the office, White agreed to meet him. Tim Conner wanted to meet out where he was looking at some property to develop. Whether Billy was too greedy to turn down an insurance sale, as Sylvia once

Welcome to Kinston, North Carolina. *Courtesy of Cathy Pickens.*

unflatteringly described him, or whether he felt obligated, given his large family responsibilities, Billy hadn't built his agency by shunning clients. He would meet clients when and where they needed him.

He likely didn't anticipate just how remote and lonely the meeting spot was. He couldn't know that Tim Conner was a false name created by James Lynwood Taylor. And he certainly didn't expect Taylor to be accompanied by Ernest Basden and a shotgun.

The next morning, when Billy still hadn't come home, Sylvia called the Lenoir County Sheriff's Office to report him missing. The sheriff, a personal friend of Billy's, knew something was wrong. Being gone overnight wasn't like Billy. Sylvia told the sheriff about the new client and where they were meeting—she had taken the phone call herself.

An aerial search spotted Billy's red minivan and directed searchers to its location, where a rural state road intersected an unpaved, rough-cut logging road surrounded by scrub brush and seed trees left after a timber harvest. The patrol cars parked near the van. Billy White lay face up, his button-down shirt covered in blood.

Oddly, Billy was the second insurance agent shot in Kinston in less than two months. In November 1992, agent Rosalyn Gray was shot to death in her driveway. Her husband, dentist Dr. William Robert Gray Jr., was charged with her murder. What was going on in the domestic lives of Kinston's insurance agents?

The small-town rumor mill buzzed. Then a tip to CrimeStoppers—coincidentally, one of many local organizations for which Billy White had volunteered—gave police a substantive lead.

Police investigations often find that all's not what it seems behind closed doors in lots of families. That was true for the Whites' blended family. Years earlier, on June 21, 1973, only eighteen months after they married, Sylvia had raced into the emergency room with Billy's youngest son, four-year-old Billy Jr., known as Little Bill. He was blue around the lips and soon pronounced dead.

Emergency room personnel found a piece of plastic, the kind dry cleaners used to cover clean clothes, so deep in his throat they couldn't see it without using a laryngoscope. The physician had to use a clamp to reach in and pull it free. Two ER nurses were suspicious that day, but according to the court record, neither pushed the matter at the time. The death was ruled accidental.

Billy Jr. had been chewing on plastic lately, his distraught stepmom told the neighbors who streamed into the house bringing casseroles and consolation. Sitting in her tidy house, receiving neighbors, she was the picture of grief.

Not that Billy's children talked about it outside the family, but they knew a different Sylvia: the harsh stepmother of stereotype made real. And the family had other secrets. When the children were grown and the nest was emptying out, Billy reportedly started drinking more than he should, and he started gambling. Sylvia tried to keep that quiet, watch out for him so clients wouldn't lose confidence and make sure he kept bringing in good money that afforded new cars and new houses—by that time, they'd moved to a newly built two-story brick house, a step up from their house on Hodges Road.

As the investigation opened the family's fissures to gossip, her first husband had stories to tell. According to author Suzanne Barr's account, Woody Taylor told how manipulative Sylvia could be, how moody and sometimes

"It's not that hard to do. I had a stepchild once. I put a bag over its head until he stopped breathing. It was better off." – Sylvia Ipock White

Suzanne Barr

Exclusive photos inside

FEATURED ON THE DISCOVERY CHANNEL'S HOT SERIES...*The New Detectives.*

Fatal Kiss, Suzanne Barr's detailed report of the case. *Courtesy of Suzanne Barr.*

physically violent. But she wasn't without her charms. After all, with Billy White, she was on her third marriage.

For Sylvia, apparently, a good man was hard to find. Turns out, too, a good hit man was hard to find, especially in a small town where the pool of applicants was necessarily limited. For at least a year, Sylvia had been fed up with all that lay on her shoulders: five children, a measure of social standing to maintain and a workaholic husband who she said drank and gambled. She was looking for a way out, but one that wouldn't hurt her lifestyle.

She asked one of her sons if he "knew anybody." Without elaborating on how, the son later said he knew what she meant. He introduced her to Linwood Taylor in the spring of 1991. Taylor, a small-time drug dealer, later said he was taken aback by what Sylvia suggested—he was no killer. But he was also intrigued by what she'd offered: $20,000 from the $200,000 life insurance proceeds, plus Billy's Chevrolet Lumina minivan. Taylor didn't have the stomach for killing someone, but $20,000 was a lot of money.

She couldn't do it herself, Sylvia said. According to trial testimony, she'd already tried to poison him with wild berries and poisonous plants. No luck. She said it couldn't look like suicide; she'd already had one husband die that way, and another would just look suspicious.

Another not-so-secret family secret popped up again in town gossip. In June 1967, Sylvia found her second husband, Leslie Ipock, dead in the bed, shot in the head, with the gun beside him.

By December 1991, Taylor said Sylvia was badgering him. He couldn't get rid of her. Finally, he approached his uncle, Ernest Basden, about helping him. Basden was a few months younger than his nephew Taylor but looked much older. He was in poor health and had a history of drug and alcohol abuse. Basden, raised by his much older father after his mother died in a car accident, had a hardscrabble upbringing, doing the farm work as his father became less able. A psychologist later described Basden as lacking self-confidence and willing to please stronger personalities.

When Taylor suggested he kill White, Basden told him he was crazy. But Taylor had to face a relentless Sylvia. He met with Sylvia at least six times over several months. He went to his uncle again and again and finally found him in a weak spot, needing money. This time, Basden agreed—he needed $300.

Taylor came up with the idea to lure Billy White out into the country. He would claim to be a busy real estate developer in the area making a deal who didn't have time to come into White's office. Sylvia suggested they pick a rural site in neighboring Jones County, somewhere away from their home turf to confuse the police.

At 8:30 p.m. on January 20, 1992, after eating a late Sunday supper at a Kinston landmark, King's BBQ Restaurant, Billy drove out of town to meet Taylor.

Taylor introduced himself as Tim Conner. He even brought along some old blueprints to make his land developer story credible. After they got out of their cars and exchanged pleasantries on the dirt road, Taylor said he needed to go into the woods to relieve himself—all part of the plan. Basden took his cue, stepped out of the far side of the car, picked up the shotgun from where he'd put it on the ground for easy access and fired point-blank at Billy White.

Basden had forgotten to cock the shotgun. White apparently stood frozen in disbelief. Nervous, Basden cocked the shotgun and fired again, hitting White in the chest. He moved closer and fired again as White lay on the ground.

The criminal masterminds drove to town, remembered that the scene was supposed to look like a robbery and drove back to search White's pockets. They went home, burned their clothes and the spent shotgun shells in the backyard, sawed up the shotgun, sealed it in a bucket filled with cement and tossed it off a bridge into the nearby Neuse River.

One week later, Sylvia had a $1,500 down payment ready for Taylor when he came to her house. She had visitors stopping by to offer condolences. They surely wondered who this unknown man was, but Taylor said he and Sylvia were discreet about the exchange of the envelope.

Taylor had promised Basden he would take all the blame if they were caught, but of course they never expected to get caught. Sylvia was so sure of herself, so certain this would work. After all, she said she'd done it before. She said she'd put a plastic bag over the head of Billy Jr. eighteen years earlier. "Not that hard," she told Taylor. "It was better off." (Not "he"; in a telling slip, she called her little blond stepson "it.")

King's BBQ, where Billy White ate his last meal, serving eastern-style pork barbecue since 1936. *Courtesy of Cathy Pickens.*

The whole story unraveled in three quick weeks once investigators got the CrimeStoppers tip to look at Taylor. At first, Taylor admitted he'd done it. When they started talking death penalty, his story flipped quickly to the truth. By then, his uncle had already confessed to his involvement. Family had told Basden he needed to talk to SBI special agent Eric Wayne Smith himself, to get his story on the record, so things would go better for him.

The Past Returns

As soon as they arrested Sylvia, investigators also began looking into the deaths of Billy Jr. and her second husband, Leslie Ipock, twenty-five years earlier. Over the years, the rumors had been faint but persistent. The thirty-two-year-old Ipock had been depressed and had been hospitalized, complaining of numbness in his extremities. Although no toxicology testing was mentioned in later reports, those symptoms had to raise questions about poisoning, but no charges were brought.

The death of Billy Jr. was a different story. In July 1992, five months after Sylvia's arrest and nineteen years after the child's death, his casket arrived at the Office of the Chief Medical Examiner in Chapel Hill. The pathologist, Dr. John Butts, examined the body and found a large, weeks-old fracture at the back of the skull. The fracture could have happened from a "serious fall onto a hard surface from a considerable distance," or he could have been hit in the back of the head with a "blunt object with considerable force."

Although the fracture didn't contribute to his death, the blow that caused it could have knocked him out and would certainly have caused a painful knot. Dr. Butt's noted the fracture was severe enough "it would be surprising if the injury that caused it was not part of the child's [medical] history." In other words, a child with a knot like that would ordinarily have been taken to a doctor. No mention was found in his medical records.

Just before his death, Billy Jr. had severely burned his legs playing with the outdoor grill. Sylvia told a friend that Billy Jr. was pulling off pieces of the plastic used to wrap the wounds and chewing on it. In the later investigation, the treating physician, Dr. Frederick Payne Dale, said he'd used a light bandage; plastic wrap would have encouraged infection, and he certainly hadn't suggested that, no matter what Sylvia said.

In reviewing the report from Lenoir County Hospital, written at the time of the child's death, Dr. Butts agreed that Billy Jr. died from asphyxia, but from "the description of the bag being wedged deeply into the throat itself, I am of the opinion that this could not have been an accidental event. Accidental asphyxias in children are caused by small objects easily inhaled or swallowed and typically occur in smaller children. I do not believe a child of this age could intentionally force a plastic bag of the size described that deep into his airway."

Much of the investigation and testimony centered on the size of the wad of plastic, the gag reflex in children and the mechanism of swallowing. After Billy Jr. was pronounced dead, the ER nurse insisted on getting the plastic out. She couldn't stand the thought of it being left in his throat. The nurse took it from the doctor. She later testified that the wadded plastic, cupped in her hand, unfolded large enough to fill her palm.

Billy White Jr. died on June 21, 1973. Sylvia was indicted for his death on September 28, 1992, more than nineteen years later.

The Trials

Because publicity and gossip naturally circled in the small town, Sylvia's trial for Billy Jr.'s death was moved sixty miles away to Williamston, in Martin County. Jury selection and opening statements started on April 12, 1993.

In the five-day trial, Dr. Page Hudson, North Carolina's chief medical examiner, testified in detail about his autopsy findings. He concurred with his colleague Dr. Butts that a child that age could not swallow something that large and pliable. The natural gag reflex and the squishiness of the plastic film would prevent it.

On April 16, 1993, the jury took less than two hours to find Sylvia guilty of her stepson's death. The judge pronounced a life sentence that day before he adjourned court.

Ernest Basden was the first to go to trial for the death of Billy White Sr., one month before Sylvia was convicted in Billy Jr.'s death. The venue was changed to Duplin County, again because of the pretrial publicity.

On the stand, Basden admitted he shot Billy White. Basden's jury took an hour and fifteen minutes to convict him. Its deliberation about his sentence took nine hours. In its recommendation to the judge, the jury found one aggravating factor that supported a tougher sentence: he'd killed for money. But it also found several factors argued for less culpability: his mental and emotional state, his remorse and acceptance of responsibility, the stress he was under at the time of the crime, his cooperation with police, his character and conduct before the murder and his religious belief and practice in prison. The judge heard the jury's long-deliberated findings and sentenced Basden to death.

In Billy Sr.'s death, Basden was the only conspirator to go to trial and the only one sentenced to death. Sylvia and Taylor took plea deals.

In November, Linwood Taylor accepted a plea deal rather than risk the death penalty at trial. His assistance in the investigation won him some leniency—a life sentence. Two years later, in December 1995, Sylvia pleaded

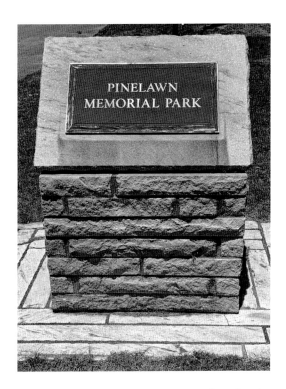

Pinelawn Memorial Park in Kinston. *Photo by Cathy Pickens.*

guilty to her husband's death. She got a second life sentence, the first for the little son and the second for the father.

Death penalty opponents fought against Basden's execution. Several jurors signed a statement saying they would have supported a sentence of life without parole if that had been an option at the time. Given arguments about the poor quality of Basden's trial representation, the head of the North Carolina Academy of Trial Lawyers argued that the new higher standards for attorneys handling capital cases should be used for any inmates currently on Death Row.

Despite the arguments, Basden's appeals failed. He was executed on December 6, 2003, the twenty-second North Carolina execution following the 1976 death penalty reinstatement.

As of 2019, Sylvia was in her early eighties and had been in prison for more than twenty-five years, serving two life sentences for the suffocation death her four-year-old stepson, Billy Jr., and for hiring Ernest Basden to kill Billy White Sr.

While blogs and online posts about crime cases abound, few include comments from those who've been inside with a convicted killer. In a blog comment on the Sylvia White case, a woman anonymously posted in 2018,

"I was locked up with her for almost 7 months in the Raleigh prison and let me tell you this woman scares me. She is sooo mean still at the age she is." A few months later, another anonymous comment echoed the sentiment: "She's still as crazy and mean as hell....Slept right beside her...and she terrified me. Threatening my life many times."

As of 2018, Sylvia had appeared before the state's parole board eight times. Eight times, she was denied parole. Billy White's daughter appeared at every hearing, making sure the board knows that family members still grieve.

Billy White and his little son were interred next to each other in Kinston's Pinelawn Memorial Park. Ernest Basden lies in the same cemetery. Sylvia's headstone is waiting for her, next to her second husband, Leslie Ipock. Even though questions persist about his suicide, Sylvia was never charged in his death.

BAD SCIENCE

Arson

Living in a rural county or a small town in the South has its attractions, but it can also be limiting. Neighbors learn about one another, make assumptions and are sometimes unwilling to allow someone to move past mistakes. Those prejudgments can set like cement and outweigh any presumption of innocence.

Before the Storm

For Terri Hinson, Columbus County and Tabor City were home, where too many people knew she'd gotten pregnant too young. But she was getting herself settled on a better course in 1993, enrolled at Southeastern Community College in Whiteville. In May 1995, she had a new baby boy, Joshua Cade, who joined older sister Brittany, age three.

In her college classes, Terri met Rodney Strickland, a fellow criminal justice major eighteen years older than she; he was a Vietnam vet who worked in construction. What started as a friendship, sharing the challenges of adults returning to college and juggling real life, became the next happy milestone in Terri's life. Rodney Strickland popped the question at Christmas 1995. In May 1996, they rented an 1,100-square-foot two-story house on Wall Street in Tabor City. Built in 1935, that house reportedly had been the first starter rental for several young marriages over the years.

Like a lot of older properties, the house needed repairs, especially to a leak in the roof, but Terri and her two children were happy with the yard, the space and the sense of being settled as a family.

Four months after they moved in, Hurricane Fran hit the North Carolina coast along the Cape Fear River. On September 5, the Category 3 storm pummeled Wilmington with 137-mile-per-hour winds. The region had suffered a hit from Hurricane Bertha only two months before, so Fran hit already damaged areas, its hurricane-force winds reaching Raleigh and flooding from South Carolina into Virginia and Ohio. Because of the severity of the storm, "Fran" was retired from the list of future hurricane names.

One month after the storm, Rodney spent the night with his mother and his youngest son in Fair Bluff, less than twenty miles away from Tabor City. At home, Terri prepared for the coldest night of the year. The temperature would drop to thirty-nine degrees that night. She plugged in two space heaters, one upstairs and one downstairs, and pulled out the blankets for their beds.

In later interviews, Terri's version of the horror scene that night never varied. As the sole eyewitness inside the house, what she saw would become critical in re-creating what happened.

Brittany's cries woke Terri—she was scared and calling for her mommy. Journalist Ann Saker recounted what Terri saw: the dark house, the stairwell to the bedrooms glowing orange. Upstairs, she ran into a wall of smoke. She could just make out Josh's crib under the window of his bedroom. Then the scene changed in an instant, as Saker reported Terri's description: "Whoosh! The fire burst from the closet in Josh's room, flame rolling across the ceiling like the ocean upside down. Smoke filled Brittany's bedroom, and Terri could not see her. She called to Brittany to follow her voice, but her daughter never appeared. The fire grew larger and hotter."

The description of the wall of smoke hanging in the room, the sudden whoosh of flame rolling across the ceiling and the heat that kept her back would all be meaningful, but only to an expert with an up-to-date understanding of fire science.

In the moment, all Terri knew was that she couldn't get to her children. She ran downstairs to call 911. Response time was almost immediate. Two police officers pulled up and found Terri on her front porch, begging them

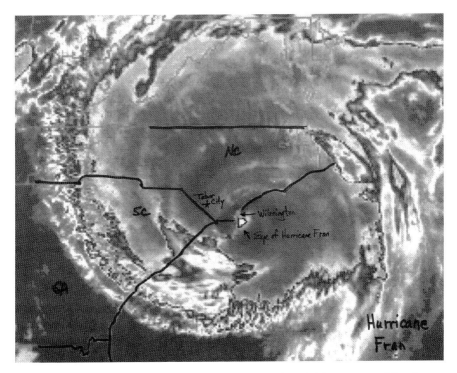

Hurricane Fran makes landfall. Arrow points to Tabor City; brighter spot to right of arrow is the eye near Wilmington. *Photo by National Oceanic and Atmospheric Administration, enhanced by author.*

to save her babies. The officers couldn't get inside. Firefighters quickly arrived and went upstairs wearing breathing gear; another climbed a ladder outside Josh's room. The heat was so intense that he crouched beneath the window frame as he sprayed water into the bedroom. Another firefighter directed water to the hole burning in the roof.

Brittany was carried out first, limp and soot-covered. Josh was located four or five minutes later. Brittany, age four, was airlifted to the Medical University of South Carolina in Charleston. Her lungs were damaged and her condition was dire. Josh, only eighteen months old, died that night. Brittany surprised some who'd seen her that night. They hadn't expected her to survive, but she was released from the hospital a week later, a resilient little girl.

Then the second horror hit Terri and her family: investigators had been busy in Tabor City.

The Investigation

As soon as they could enter the burned house, the city fire chief and the chief of police combed through the rubble looking for what started the fire. In Josh's bedroom, the fire chief spotted a V-shaped burn pattern on the wall, pointing to a pile of burned clothing on the floor. He knew from his experience that V-shaped burn patterns point to the origin of a fire. Long before the chief had started working fires, fire investigators knew what that meant.

From their first look, the investigators believed the fire had been deliberately set. If that was true, the most logical culprit was the mother who'd been home with her children that night—the same mother who'd run out and left her children in the flames.

The local officials called the State Bureau of Investigation for help. The SBI called in the Charlotte office of the federal Bureau of Alcohol, Tobacco and Firearms. They studied the scene carefully. The closet was an addition to the room, built of half-inch plywood and one-inch tongue-in-groove pine. The fire burned a hole in the ceiling over the closet; a closet shelf showed more fire damage on the bottom than on the top. The investigators agreed the fire started in the pile of clothes and then burned the shelf bottom, moving upward and making the hole into the attic.

Upstairs in the attic, they noted old fabric-wrapped electrical wiring, probably installed when the house was built in the 1930s. They concurred that the fire started in Josh's closet. They found no electrical or other accidental cause for the fire. It had to be arson.

They also found witnesses from the scene that night who said that Terri didn't act right. She wasn't emotional enough. Investigators learned she'd had some youthful indiscretions and had even given up her three older children for adoption after the end of her first marriage. She explained that, at her mother's urging, she'd done what was best for her children because she couldn't adequately care for them financially. The investigators weren't convinced. What kind of mother would give away her children? They felt certain they were looking at someone who'd burned her house down with her two remaining children in it.

Brittany miraculously left the hospital a week after the fire. The Department of Social Services, charged with protecting children at risk, surprised her family by arriving at the hospital and taking Brittany away from her mother. The shock was only slightly lessened when a judge later agreed to let Brittany stay with Terri's mom, Bernice Prince.

On November 20, one month after the fire and three weeks after her surviving daughter was taken from her, North Carolina State Bureau of Investigation special agent Matt White arrested thirty-two-year-old Terri Hinson for first-degree murder and first-degree arson. In North Carolina, the penalty could be death or life in prison.

Terri's attorney managed to get her released on a $200,000 bond, extremely rare in a capital murder case. Her family struggled but raised the bail bond fee. She was confined by an ankle monitor to house arrest and not allowed to attend church. Her young daughter could visit her two afternoons per week. She could visit her son's grave once a week and work with her lawyer on her case. The slow march of the investigation and the specter of a trial consumed her life.

The judge allotted funds for her defense to hire an independent fire investigator. Unfortunately for Terri, the hired defense investigator agreed with the state investigators: the fire was arson and caused by Terri Hinson, the only person with access to the site of the fire that night. Her case grew even bleaker.

Terri, to keep busy at home, kept books for Rodney's construction business. She got advice by phone from a clerk at Fayetteville's Circuit City and used her credit card to buy a $2,500 Compaq computer to help her handle the job. That was more than the $1,500 the state had paid for the fire expert who didn't help her, but this would be money well spent.

She'd taken a college computer class, but that didn't include anything about the internet. She taught herself how to use Weblink's internet service, logged on and began her own investigation. With a dial-up modem and lots of persistence, she searched for anything related to fire and arson.

"They're Always Getting It Wrong"

Without the internet, she would never have found Tony Cafe, a fire investigator in Sydney, Australia, or read his article on the importance of laboratory chemical analysis to determine whether a fire is accident or arson.

Anne Saker reported Terri's e-mail exchange: "Did Cafe know of any cases when a fire investigator got it wrong? Cafe responded the next day. Sure, he wrote, they're always getting it wrong."

Cafe put her in touch with Dr. Gerald Hurst in Austin, Texas. Terri wrote and told him, "A lady's life is in jeopardy." She couldn't know, when she hit "Send," just how right Hurst was for the job. Hurst fit the description of eccentric mad scientist. According to reporter Saker, he developed trade secret or patented formulas for a second-generation Liquid Paper, Mylar balloons and a popular two-part explosive called Kinepak. With his Doctor of Philosophy degree in chemistry from Cambridge University and his experience with rockets and explosives, he had the requisite training to explain the science of fires. Terri wasn't the first accused arsonist who'd come to Hurst for help.

In his e-mails to Terri, Hurst showed an unscientific compassion. Over time, he meticulously drew from her descriptions of important elements—the weather before the fire, what she'd observed, what the experts observed—and he filtered it through all his experiences with fire. As Saker reported, "From more than 1,000 miles away, the fire looked accidental to Hurst."

Hurst brought more than just his technical know-how to Terri's case. Even though he met Terri early in his career of accepting *pro bono* cases for those wrongly accused, Hurst understood the typical path such an investigation would take, starting with outdated old-wives' tales called "science," followed by demonizing the supposed arsonist (often a mother), as well as her character, her actions and reactions to the fire and the deaths.

Terri's case followed the path Hurst expected, and he prepared her for what would come. Hurst, in quiet, calm e-mail statements, reassured her: "You are not responsible." And he encouraged her to live her life without worrying about others' opinions.

With his advice in mind, on December 23, 1997, after being engaged for two years, Terri married Rodney Strickland. Terri chose one of Brittany's scheduled visitation days so she could be the maid of honor. Locked away with her ankle monitor and her Compaq computer, Terri found Dr. Hurst's e-mails and his measured, sensible approach refreshing.

Finally, one of Terri's attorneys officially invited Hurst to participate in her defense. Hurst prepared a detailed opinion letter for attorney William Wood, dated March 16, 1998. In the letter, Hurst pulled no punches, outlining what he found in the fire scene photos and the mistakes the state's investigators made, all based on outdated fire science.

For decades, each new generation of fire investigators had learned from the old guys. They learned that Vs pointed to where a fire started because heat rises and fires burn up, not down; that concrete spalls and window glass crazes from high heat, indicating that an accelerant was used. Too seldom did they learn that the only way to accurately identify accelerants is in a chemistry lab or the importance of eliminating all possible accidental causes before deciding on arson. Arson couldn't be proved with a cursory review of wiring or appliances or the background of the homeowner, but rather with evidence collected and studied in a lab.

Into the 1980s, fire investigators' old-boys' tales had been gathered and published as definitive guidelines. In 1985, though, seasoned investigators began to push for more scientific analysis of "the way we've always done it" techniques. The National Fire Protection Association published *NFPA 921: Guide for Fire and Explosion Investigations* in 1992.

Many old-line fire investigators weren't pleased. This turned everything they knew upside down. What prompted the change? In 1990, fire investigators John Lentini and John DeHaan had an epiphany. They were studying a fire scene in Marietta, Georgia, and saw burn and pour patterns they believed indicated arson. Unlike most fire scenes, though, this time they had access to an identical unoccupied house next door. They were allowed to install the same sofa and furnishings and set that house on fire without accelerant.

That test fire changed modern fire investigation. In less than five minutes, dramatically faster than conventional wisdom taught was possible, the smoke and heat in the room built to a flashover point—the point where an entire room bursts into flames.

What became known as the "Lime Street fire" experiment demonstrated that flashover changes everything about a fire scene. All the rules used to interpret a scene changed as soon as flashover occurred. A post-flashover scene had to be read very differently than a pre-flashover scene. And even without accelerant, flashover could happen quickly.

One year later, Lentini and others got a fire investigator's idea of a dream laboratory. A destructive brush fire outside Oakland, California, consumed three thousand houses and killed more than two dozen people. Choosing fifty of those houses to study, they found arson indicators where they knew, without doubt, no accelerants were used, where arson clearly hadn't occurred.

Lentini was especially curious about the phenomenon of crazed window glass. The spider-webbing on glass panes had long been considered a sign of arson and high temperatures only possible with an accelerant. As with much of the common wisdom, this assumption had never been subjected to lab testing. He found that when he heated up different types of glass, none of it crazed. When he sprayed it with water, it all crazed. In an *ABA Journal* interview, Lentini said, "The only thing crazed glass tells you is that the glass got hot and the fire department came and put out the fire."

By 2000, the new *NFPA 921* had become the "generally accepted" standard for fire investigators. The percentage of fires identified as arson dropped from 15 percent to 6 percent. But that affected only jurisdictions where fire investigators kept current with changes in the field. Two weeks after Hurst submitted his opinion letter, Hurst and Terri's defense lawyers sat down with the prosecutor to review his report.

In Hurst's methodically worded ten-page letter, in language with enough detail to satisfy an expert but clear enough for a layman to understand, Hurst said none of the accepted signs of arson was present (incendiary devices, ignitable liquids); damaged wiring in the attic, combined with the roof leak and the storm, likely created an arc to flammable shredded-newsprint insulation; and the fire most likely started in the attic, the most damaged part of the house.

The hole in the closet ceiling came not from clothes on the floor burning upward. Instead, the smoldering attic fire burned through to the closet, dropping flaming material onto the pile of clothes, which then burned back upward. As discussed in *NFPA 921*, "The investigator should keep in mind that during the progress of a fire, burning debris often falls to lower levels and then burns upward from there." Hurst believed that "falldown" or "dropdown" ignited the clothes, which then burned the V pattern mistaken for the source. He also believed that the smoldering clothes and wood in the closet created the "smokehouse effect"—the wall of smoke Terri saw hovering above the floor of the room when she tried to enter.

Fire investigators had pointed to damage on the bottom of the closet shelf as more evidence that the clothes had been set on fire. Hurst said the bottom of shelf burned because nothing protected it. Folded clothes, a new box of six drinking glasses and a popcorn tin on top of the shelf insulated it from damage, as well as added more evidence consistent with dropdown from the attic.

Hurst also addressed the common tactic of "demonizing the defendant" to help build an arson case. He pointed out that far from being an indictment of Terri and her feelings for her children, the "fact that Ms. Hinson had previously allowed the adoption of three children in a period of financial difficulty is proof enough that she would have been easily able to find her child a suitable home had she wished to free herself from responsibility."

According to reporter Anne Saker, in meeting with the prosecution and defense, Dr. Hurst asked questions and SBI investigator Matt White answered:

"Why did you think it was arson?" / "Because of the fire pattern in the closet."
"Did you look in the attic?" / "That was not the point of origin."
"How do you know that?" / "The point of origin was in the closet."

Although White pointed to the V-shaped pattern, he also agreed that a fire starting in the closet would have burned through the thin plywood closet and into the bedroom before burning through the one-inch ceiling and into the attic. The two-hour conversation was polite. The state's investigator didn't waver. The prosecutor listened.

Prosecutor Lee Bollinger later said he didn't want to rush into dropping charges. The state had spent a lot of time building its case. State investigators with a lot of experience were involved. Bollinger took time to study the *NFPA 921* fire investigation guide. He watched one-inch pine tongue-in-groove board burn. He talked to the landlord's insurance company and found that its investigators still had the section of wire they cut from the attic; Hurst's report had noted it was missing. Bollinger knew he could take the case to the jury, but he himself saw reasonable doubt about Terri's guilt.

For Terri and her family, it was a painful wait while the prosecutor digested and double-checked the information Hurst had supplied, but finally, a little over two weeks later, Bollinger dropped the charges. He said the electrical cable in the attic couldn't be eliminated as the cause of the electrical fire, but as Hurst and the latest standards noted, if accident can't be ruled out, a fire shouldn't be automatically ruled arson.

By the time charges were dropped, Terri had spent seventeen months under house arrest. Unfortunately for her, some of her neighbors and the investigators who'd built the case against her weren't as willing to step back from their now strongly held belief that she'd killed her son and tried to kill her daughter. Some had invested too much time and career credibility; others had limited information but believed the story woven about the bad mama. For whatever reason, the logical, science-based arguments of Gerald Hurst didn't penetrate the deeply held prejudices of some in law enforcement and in Columbus County.

After the Lime Street fire prompted increasingly scientific fire scene investigations, a group of experienced arson investigators gathered for training at the Federal Law Enforcement Training Center in 1993. The participants were asked to identify the quadrant of the room (not the exact spot) where a fire started. Edward Humes summarized the results in his book *Burned*: "Some of the nation's leading local arson investigators, asked to identify where a fire started in an empty room, failed to do so more than nine out of ten times."

In general, faulty forensic evidence leads to one-fourth of the wrongful convictions later overturned. A 90 percent arson test failure rate is even more alarming than the 70 percent failure rate in bad eyewitness cases.

Hurst continued to use his time and expertise to fight long-accepted but erroneous fire "science," but not always with success. In 2004, Hurst got involved in one of his best-known cases, more than a decade after a deadly Texas fire and during the frenzied last days before the convicted arsonist's scheduled execution. In December 1991, Cameron Todd Willingham was convicted in Texas for setting the fire that killed his three daughters. He said he was home asleep when the fire started and always maintained his innocence. The case followed the pattern Hurst had become so familiar with: demonizing the parent/suspected arsonist, use of outdated fire "science" and assessments that the parent's responses at and after the fire were inappropriate.

In 2004, Hurst submitted a detailed report of the errors to Texas governor Rick Perry and the Board of Pardon and Parole. The report was received but not acknowledged. The execution was carried out on February 17, 2004.

A series of investigations followed, including an investigative report by the *Chicago Tribune*, a *New Yorker* article by David Grann and investigations by Barry Scheck's Innocence Project and by John Lentini and other experts. The conclusion? The fire science was bad, along the same lines as the errors in Terri Hinson's case. Todd Willingham was innocent, as he'd always said he was. The initiating point for the turning tide in his case was Gerald Hurst's report. For Willingham, though, it did not land on the desk of anyone willing to listen before it was too late.

The result in the Willingham case brings home Terri Hinson's good fortune in having an open-minded prosecutor willing to seek truth, not just convictions. The investment of time, resources and ego provide plenty of reasons not to reconsider. Thanks to both Gerald Hurst's methodical persuasiveness and prosecutor Lee Bollinger's openness, Terri Hinson's case had a very different outcome from Todd Willingham's.

Gerald Hurst died in March 2015, from complications of a prior liver transplant that had given him many more years than expected. During those extra years, Hurst reviewed countless cases of suspected arson. For cases like Terri's, he didn't charge for his opinion. In cases where his review clearly indicated arson, he told attorneys they didn't want a written opinion from him—their clients needed to accept a plea deal. In the other cases, Hurst fought to reeducate and persuade outdated experts.

After her release, Terri and her husband thought about leaving the Tabor City area, but that was hard to do, with family and friends there.

Terri lived only fifteen years after her ordeal. She passed away at age forty-nine. Her daughter posted a Facebook update four years later, in 2017, saying, "Yes, I am the same Brittany Hinson that was in the very well known house fire in Tabor City." People sometimes looked for her online and wanted to know how things turned out for her. Befitting a case where online searches averted a tragic prosecution and likely conviction and where harsh online comments brought continued pain to those affected by the fire that night, online searches also, perhaps a little, reminded a daughter that others out there cared and wished her well.

More Bad Science

Most law enforcement and forensics professionals work diligently to seek justice—whether that search ends in convicting a wrongdoer or exonerating an innocent person. When one of those justice-seekers puts a finger on the scale to weigh it toward a particular outcome, all of us suffer—none, though, as severely as those wrongly accused.

Just why would a justice-seeker veer off the path? Because it moves a case off the desk? Because of personal conviction that the accused is guilty even though the proof is hard to find? Because of fear of professional repercussions for allowing a case to collapse because you can't find the evidence? Because of hubris or a god complex? In trying to understand how those charged with finding and proving "truth" can be untruthful, the reasons are sometimes obscure.

Cutting-Edge Analysis

In the case of Dr. Louise Robbins, the reasons are obscure and the outcomes are frightening. Perhaps it was nothing more than professional ambition and pride. Perhaps it was a significant failure in the checks and balances in our legal system, allowing "scientific" evidence that had not met the rigors of scientific peer-reviewed evaluation. Whatever the reasons, the case of North Carolina's footprint expert, with her "Cinderella analysis," is bizarre indeed.

One strength of our jury system is that ordinary folks sit and listen to witnesses, watch their demeanor, see how they hold up to cross-examination by attorneys on the other side and make their collective decision about what they believe and what they don't.

If two people who witness a car accident have different perceptions of what happened, ordinary people get to listen and judge. Sometimes, though, the testimony falls outside jurors' everyday experience. Sometimes jurors need to hear from experts—maybe an expert on accident data recorded on "black boxes" in modern cars, how cell towers register the location of calls or how doctors are supposed to perform a knee surgery. An attorney presents the expert's credentials, and the judge decides whether that expert is qualified to give an opinion. In assessing an expert, the judge's discretion is absolute and won't be overturned unless an appellate court finds "no evidence to support it." In other words, judges serve as absolute gatekeepers when witness testimony is specialized and outside the everyday expertise of jurors.

The standard judges should use to measure an expert's credentials was first spelled out in *Frye v. U.S.*, a 1923 Supreme Court case debating an early version of the polygraph. The court said finding the line between "experimental and demonstrable" was hazy, but courts couldn't hang back in the Dark Ages. The *Frye* test let judges push the boundaries when the scientific evidence was "sufficiently established to have gained general acceptance in the particular field." In *Frye*, the judge said the polygraph wasn't scientifically reliable enough in 1923 to be admitted; polygraph exams are still not held reliable enough to be admissible.

The work of a North Carolina academic anthropologist would challenge the *Frye* test, although it took a while. In 1976, Dr. Louise Robbins, on the faculty at the University of North Carolina–Greensboro, stepped outside her classroom and into a courtroom as an expert witness on footprint identification. To testify, Dr. Robbins first had to convince judges that her evidence was "sufficiently established" and generally accepted in her field.

She told judges she'd done what most academic physical anthropologists do: she worked at archaeological digs, studied human skeletons, identified an area of specialty and began having her students at UNC–Greensboro collect footprints for her—1,200 of them. Based on her credentials, she was deemed an expert in every court where she was hired to testify.

Using data she'd gathered from her research, she delivered her opinions with authority and certainty. She took her time and carefully showed judges and jurors the visuals she used to arrive at her conclusions, so they could come to the same conclusions.

The Bullard Trial

In a 1984 North Carolina murder case against Vonnie Ray Bullard, Dr. Robbins outlined for the judge her academic qualifications, the people she'd worked with (including legendary archaeologist Mary Leakey, who asked her to study prehistoric footprints in Tanzania) and her membership in the American Academy of Forensic Sciences. She cited her article on "The Individuality of Footprints" soon to appear in the *Journal of Forensic Science*, her consultations with the FBI and testimony in four other states.

Outside the jury's hearing, the judge let her educate him on her methodology. She didn't consider the foot's ridge detail in her identifications, the process used in fingerprint identification. She didn't need that. Instead, she compared the unique shapes and sizes of impressions created by the bones of the foot, particularly the heel, arch, ball and toes. The judge deemed her qualified.

Neither she nor the judge knew it at the time, but two years later, in 1986, a special panel would be convened within the American Academy of Forensic Sciences to review her work, hoping to "be a significant factor in the prevention of serious miscarriage of justice." But that came later.

Prints from bare feet, like fingerprints, have long been used in criminal investigations because bare feet, like fingers, can show distinctive ridge detail. Shoeprint impressions have also helped link suspects to crime scenes because distinctive wear patterns on a shoe make it unique among shoes of the same make. In one notable case, prints from Bruno Magli shoes were introduced in the civil case against O.J. Simpson. Size-twelve prints from Bruno Magli Lorenzo shoes were found in blood at the scene of the murders of Nicole Brown Simpson and Ron Goldman. O.J. Simpson wore size twelve, but he denied he ever wore "those ugly-ass shoes."

No shoes were found specifically linked to Simpson or the scene. However, a photograph of Simpson wearing that brand of shoe became key evidence at the civil trial brought by the victims' families against Simpson. Typically, a *type* of shoe wouldn't be enough to link a particular wearer to a scene. In that case, though, the photograph combined with the small number of Bruno Magli Lorenzo shoes sold *and* Simpson's denial he'd ever worn them created an admissible link for the jury to consider.

What Louise Robbins could add to a trial was even more unusual than the O.J. footwear evidence. Dr. Robbins said she could match a wearer's unique footprint to any shoe in his or her closet; she didn't look at wear patterns on the shoe soles or one-of-a-kind markings such a gouge or tear. Instead, she said that an individual's foot structure makes identifiable and unique marks, no matter what shoes he wears—or even if he's barefoot but leaves no visible ridge details. She said that no one shares foot shape or gait, so everyone leaves identifiably different prints inside their shoes *and* where they walk. She had the data and charts and acetate overlays to prove it.

Dr. Robbins had attracted popular press attention when, in Africa, she announced that a footprint fossil had been made by a pregnant woman—five and a half months pregnant, to be exact. An academic colleague from the University of California–Berkeley who worked with her in Africa called that nonsense, but naysaying doesn't make as catchy a headline as a 3.5-million-year-old pregnant woman's footprint.

In a courtroom, Robbins, like the accomplished professor she was, took time to walk juries through her analysis. She showed diagrams, educating them about the physiology of the foot and its bones. Then, with unassailable confidence, she would link the print at the scene with the defendant. Unfortunately, those against whom she appeared seldom had experts on their side able to call her findings nonsense. After all, it's hard to challenge someone who is the only expert in the world.

One of the few called to rebut Dr. Robbins in cases around the country was William Bodziak, an FBI footwear impressions expert. Bodziak found himself in the unaccustomed position of testifying not for the prosecution but as an expert for defendants. He knew Dr. Robbins's claims of groundbreaking science were dangerous, and he didn't want innocent people convicted.

In Vonnie Ray Bullard's case, as the appellate court opinion noted, one thousand exhibits and eighty-one witnesses were presented, more than half of whom were named Bullard. Subtracting Dr. Louise Robbins's testimony, the jury heard plenty of others describe the long-standing animosity between Bullard and victim, Pedro Hales. Hales had shot and injured Bullard's son three years earlier. When Hales's self-defense claim got him acquitted by a jury, Vonnie Bullard vowed he'd kill him.

On the August evening Pedro disappeared, Vonnie was riding in Pedro's truck, and the two were seen arguing. Vonnie was barefoot that evening and carrying a .22-caliber handgun. At some point, Vonnie got his own truck, which was seen on Melvin's Bridge over the South River, the river where Pedro's body was found days later. On the bridge, investigators found blood, a .22-caliber bullet, bloody bare footprints on the asphalt (though no ridge detail because of the rough surface), broken glass and part of a red plastic seatbelt assembly linked to the defendant's truck. Vonnie's truck had a smear of the victim's blood inside, a broken back window and a hole in the seatbelt assembly where one would expect to find a hole from a bullet fired from the driver's seat at a passenger.

To a logical mind, Dr. Robbins's match seemed farfetched. But with all that physical evidence, who needed to match a bloody bare footprint on asphalt or sand, which showed no distinguishing ridge detail, to Vonnie Ray Bullard?

Nonetheless, the North Carolina Supreme Court found Dr. Robbins's testimony admissible and upheld Bullard's first-degree murder conviction in 1984. The appellate opinion noted, "Certainly, Dr. Robbins' testimony assisted the jury in making certain inferences about the footprints on the bridge, which could not have been made without the testimony of someone with the qualifications of Dr. Robbins."

The appellate judges were content to say of Robbins's testimony, "Let it in, let the jury decide what weight to give it." In this case, because she had diagrams and described things a jury could see for themselves, the judge said her testimony wasn't like a lie detector test, inadmissible in court because jurors couldn't understand what the machine was doing. Jurors could look at what she looked at and draw their own conclusions. She was still considered an expert, according to North Carolina courts.

However, in 1986, a 135-member panel convened by the American Academy of Forensic Sciences solely to investigate her work found her conclusions could not be duplicated by other experts and had no basis in science. Despite her visually compelling charts and convincing professorial demeanor, her work was not solid science. Before her death from brain cancer in 1987, according to debunker of bad forensics Jim Fisher, she testified in ten states and Canada; at least twelve people went to prison with help from her testimony.

Successes in forensic science command headlines, creating an aura of objective infallibility. For the sake of those wrongly accused, the inevitable fallibility of humans is worth remembering.

THE ROCKINGHAM MURDERS

Richmond County

Unwritten Law: The Ormond/Cole Case

With the passage of almost one hundred years, much stays the same in a small North Carolina town, but much also changes, which makes the 1925 murder of W.W. "Bill" Ormond on an August afternoon in downtown Rockingham a case still worth puzzling over. If the state's criminal law calls murder a crime, can a jury legitimately recognize a higher law, one allowing a father to defend the integrity of his daughter and protect his family?

The story starts when Ormond, a tall, handsome World War I veteran damaged by exposure to poison gas while fighting in the trenches in France, came home to North Carolina. His war-related hearing loss and what is now recognized as posttraumatic stress disorder made it difficult for him to continue in college classes or to get the types of office jobs to which he was once suited.

His father was a Methodist minister, serving at the Rockingham United Methodist (now First United Methodist) Church before being called to serve in Nashville, North Carolina, near Rocky Mount. Before he enlisted, Bill attended Duke University. He tried to return to North Carolina State University after the war but could not hear well enough to succeed in classes.

Left: First United Methodist Church in Rockingham. *Photo by Cathy Pickens.*

Below: Cornerstone at First United Methodist Church, showing its long history. *Photo by Cathy Pickens.*

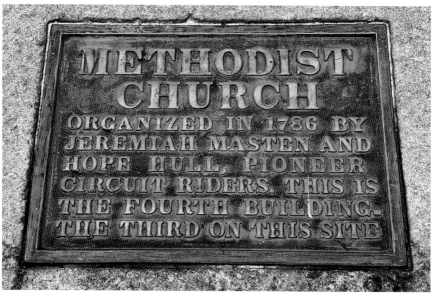

Street sign in the neighborhood once dominated by Hannah Pickett Mill, built by William Cole in 1906. *Photo by Cathy Pickens.*

Bill did, though, get a job in the physical plant at N.C. State and was quickly promoted to electrician. As he started to get himself settled into a new life, he struck up an acquaintance with and began dating Miss Elizabeth Cole. She had attended Converse College in Spartanburg, South Carolina, and was the daughter of wealthy textile magnate William Bonaparte Cole.

Bill Cole had learned to run a textile mill from hands-on experience before he gathered the financing and, in 1906, built the Hannah Pickett Mill, named to honor his great-grandmother. Twenty years later, he added Hannah Pickett No. 2. With his business acumen and knowledge of cloth-making, he became one of the wealthiest men in the region.

Bill had three children, but with his older daughter, Elizabeth—or Libbut, as he nicknamed her—he had a special bond. They'd always been buddies. At age twenty-four, she was an active and well-liked member of her circle of friends. When she started dating Bill Ormond, some probably wondered at her choice. A preacher's son with physical disabilities and no college education couldn't offer her the standard of living she had in her father's house or could have with another beau.

Elizabeth Cole and Bill Ormond kept company for two years, in the swirl of the usual ice cream socials and visits between friends' houses, before their relationship ended. Her friends and acquaintances debated the reasons. Had her father forced the split because Bill Ormond simply wasn't good enough for his daughter, as some suggested? Or, as she explained, had she figured out they had no future and she'd been the one who called it quits?

Wherever the truth lay in the end of their relationship, Bill Ormond didn't take it well. Was he heartbroken at losing her, as he said? Or at losing the promise of her father's fortune, as some gossiped? He continued to try to contact her. Then he wheeled out the big guns: he wrote a letter to Elizabeth's father. The town gossiped about the letters exchanged between the two men, but gossip would be all they had until the trial. No one who'd read them was talking.

Had the case happened almost a century later, the gossip would have circled around Facebook posts or text messages. But in 1925, those handwritten or typed letters were the center of Rockingham's attention.

As might be expected at the time, with Bill off working at the college, Elizabeth had written him a handful of letters during their courtship. Townsfolk thought the possible subject matter worth dissecting. Had she indicated they were engaged? Was she suggesting that her father stood in the way of their romance? Her words, though, weren't as interesting or as incendiary as Bill Ormond's words to her father.

The most hotly debated letter, the so-called slander letter, eventually introduced at Cole's trial, was written by Bill Ormond to Cole, addressed from N.C. State College in Raleigh. Ormond wrote:

> *Dear Mr. Cole: You have received two letters from me. One was as nice as I know how to write, and no attention was paid to it. The other one was written with no hard feelings.*
>
> *I simply tried to let you know the relation that had existed between your daughter and myself.*
>
> *…I have a feeling of pity knowing what might happen if the facts were uncovered. It is for your family I am writing this.…What would she feel like marrying someone after we have had relations as man and wife for over a year?* [He also quoted one of her letters to him:] *"Bill, I love you enough to do anything and we are going to get married soon."*

A handful of friends witnessed Cole's response to the letter, including his personal attorney, Fred Byrum. Cole shook and fainted. His discomfiture didn't abate over time, but Cole stayed very closemouthed about what the letter said—which is what set the rumor mill working wildly.

As later revealed in court testimony, as soon as he'd gathered himself from reading the shocking revelation in the letter, Cole asked Elizabeth to come meet him, and he drove them outside of town where they could talk. He assured her he would stand beside her, but if Ormond's letter were true, her only honorable action would be to marry him. "I'm not here to scold you, but to sympathize with you."

"This is a lie and absolutely untrue," she told him.

Cole continued to push the point. If this happened, they should marry. He said he'd take care of them.

As she later testified, "I told Daddy that Bill knows why we broke off. I told him that I could not marry Bill now if he was the last man on earth." She even offered to be physically examined, if her father had any doubts about her. He didn't; he trusted her word.

Chastity and the value of female honor may sound hopelessly outdated and old-fashioned now, but for Mr. Cole—and, indeed, for most god-fearing, churchgoing folks in Rockingham and elsewhere—a virtuous woman had a price beyond rubies, as the book of Proverbs declared.

The slander letter served only as the opening salvo in a flaming war of words. In his response, Cole came out blazing. "You damnable, mean, insulting cur," he wrote to Ormond. If he heard anything else about Elizabeth that came from Ormond, Cole continued, he promised to "fill your body with lead."

Ormond's response was less direct but no less combative: "You are going to chew and swallow all that cur stuff.…To call you a cur is a great compliment.…Your bluffing has come to an end." This is what a Twitter flame war would sound like if handwritten on nice notepaper.

Cole immediately sought the counsel of his attorney and friend Fred Byrum. Worried about the escalating anger, Byrum offered to go to Raleigh to talk to Ormond, to settle this war of words in person. At their meeting, with the added encouragement of Bill's father, Reverend Ormond, Byrum helped Bill Ormond craft another letter, this one an apology to Cole: "My purpose in writing threatening letters was to induce you to let me see Elizabeth." Ormond wrote that he promised to stay away from Elizabeth and to not write any more abusive letters. As a parting shot, though, he added that Cole should let his daughter marry whomever she chose.

On their drive back to Raleigh after their meeting, Byrum had to wonder why he'd gone to the trouble. On the trip, Ormond said, "If Cole ever crosses my path, I'll shoot him through." To punctuate his point, he pulled a pistol from the pocket of his car.

Today, Ormond's actions might be spotted as a warning of escalating and dangerous domestic violence, but at the time, Cole accepted the apparent truce.

The steamy, angry melodrama continued to play out with other small installments until its denouement on August 16, 1925. Despite Reverend Ormond suggesting his two sons find another driving route from Raleigh to Myrtle Beach, Ormond chose to drive through Rockingham, the very place he'd promised to avoid. He parked downtown less than a block from the Manufacturers Building, where Cole kept his office. Ormond had spent part of the day at Ledbetter's Pond with friends and then drove into town to make phone arrangements to visit Miss Laura Steele, Elizabeth's cousin.

Ledbetter's Pond, a longtime favorite outdoor spot near Rockingham. *Photo by Cathy Pickens.*

Manufacturers Building in downtown Rockingham, location of William Cole's office. *Photo by Cathy Pickens.*

After the phone call, Ormond returned to his Ford roadster, sat in the front seat and lit a cigarette. Bill Cole saw him. Mindful of the threats that Ormond would shoot him on sight and mindful of reports that Ormond kept a pistol in his car, often on the front seat, Cole went to his car and retrieved his own handgun.

Witnesses said Cole approached Ormond's roadster from behind, where Ormond couldn't easily see him. Cole drew up even with the side of the car, reached in and fired. Cole himself testified that Ormond grabbed the barrel of the pistol. Cole feared he would twist it from his hand. He fired twice more at close range. He then walked the few yards back to his office.

Witnesses carried Ormond to a nearby doctor's office, where he died. Cole drove home and waited for the sheriff. If anyone doubted Cole's influence in the region and in North Carolina, the deputy sheriff wasn't one of the doubters. He placed a call to Raleigh to W.J. Adams, a judge on the North Carolina Supreme Court. The judge assured him that Cole needed to be arrested.

No one reported that Cole made any protest about his arrest. His attorneys chose not to seek bail. Although friends did bring a bed to make his cell more comfortable, his attorneys had it removed. They wanted to avoid any appearance of favoritism or subversion of the course of justice.

Awaiting trial, Cole was held in the jail at the back of the Richmond County Courthouse, where he could walk about in the building. Friends and associates could visit, and he continued to conduct business while incarcerated.

Did Ormond have a gun in his car? That key question wasn't easily answered, as it turned out. Ormond made a point of letting Cole and others know he always had a gun with him, but where was it after the shooting? The police later received the gun, and the most plausible story is that a friend found the gun, either on the seat or in the pocket of Ormond's car, and took it to Laura Steele. The reported emissary for its return to authorities was Laura's wealthy aunt, Miss Fannie Steele.

The Trial

A special court session was ordered for the trial of William Bonaparte Cole in the week of September 28, 1925, scarcely one month after the shooting. A stunning seventeen lawyers filled the tables at the front of the courtroom, for the prosecution and the defense.

Ormond's defense team included a past commander of the North Carolina American Legion. According to author John Hutchinson, even though newspapers reported that James Lockhart would work for the family of war veteran Ormond, the lawyer instead joined Cole's team.

Ormond's family and friends, wanting to bolster a prosecution that faced the kind of defense money and influence could buy, built their own dream team, including a man who'd recently studied at Yale under former president William Howard Taft and another who would sit as a judge at the Nuremberg trials.

Court watchers clambered to see Elizabeth Cole on the stand and hear what she had to say. The *Gastonia Gazette* reported that she was "a far prettier girl than Converse College pictures show her to be." She testified that she'd broken off her relationship with Bill Ormond in the fall of 1924 and that her father had shown her a letter in February 1925, the now much-rumored slander letter. Court watchers reported she was calm during her testimony. Her father, though, showed his only bouts of nervousness as she sat on the stand.

Cole couldn't claim that he didn't shoot Ormond. Instead, his attorneys claimed that he acted in self-defense, protecting himself and his family. Although Ormond had issued threats and had shown up in town when he'd promised to stay away, the trouble with a self-defense argument was that Cole was the one who approached with a gun. Ormond didn't have time to pull his gun, assuming he had one with him.

Many pundits argued that his defense relied on a notion of an "unwritten law" that a man had an obligation and right to protect his family from damaging insult as well as physical harm. In case his self-defense claim failed, Cole's lawyers had a fallback: "transitory insanity," in which he was so overwrought by the threats and the tensions and his worry that Ormond would kill him and leave his family without a defender that he was rendered temporarily insane. He was currently sane and able to tell right from wrong, but he was insane in that moment in downtown Rockingham. Of course, newspapers from around the region and as far away as Atlanta and Cleveland hooted over that legal strategy.

Those extralegal arguments, though, had a precedent, one with an odd connection to the Carolinas. From 1865 to 1867, Union general Daniel Sickles from New York served as the military governor of both North Carolina and South Carolina. A political opportunist, he had served in Congress, had been New York City's corporate counsel aiding the land acquisition for Central Park and had won his generalship by political appointment, not by battlefield valor. In fact, he'd lost a leg at Gettysburg after disobeying an order. But Sickles's ascendancies and falls in military and political arenas are not what make him memorable decades later. He is more famous for getting away with murder.

On February 27, 1859, on a residential street in Washington, he shot Philip Barton Key to death. Tall, charming district attorney Key, the son of Francis Scott Key of "The Star-Spangled Banner" fame, had become increasingly friendly with Sickles's beautiful but lonely wife, Teresa Bagioli Sickles—so friendly that Washington tongues began to wag with tales. As

Major General Daniel E. Sickles, officer of the Federal army. *Courtesy of Civil War Photographs, 1861–1865, Library of Congress, Prints and Photographs Division.*

THE TRIAL OF THE HON. DANIEL K. SICKLES FOR THE MURDER OF P. BARTON KEY, ESQ., AT WASHINGTON, D.C.

Trial of Daniel Sickles for the murder of Philip Barton Key, from *Harper's Weekly*, April 9, 1859. *Courtesy of Library of Congress, Prints and Photographs Division.*

Sickles inveigled and intrigued his way around Washington, his own marital peccadilloes failed to attract the gossip his wife's did.

As in the Ormond case, the waters were roiled by a letter, this one anonymous, letting Sickles know of his wife's company-keeping at a house "on 15th Street bt'w'n K and L Streets." After forcing Teresa to confess, Sickles accosted Key on a city street and shot him three times. Key was unarmed.

Sickles's case marks the first significant use of self-defense in a U.S. murder trial. As in the Ormond case, Sickles's defense was bolstered by the unwritten law: the right to avenge familial honor. The jury let Sickles walk free. He continued a diplomatic career and lived to age ninety-three. Teresa died eight years after the trial, at about age thirty.

The Sickles case did not set legal precedent for the unwritten law, but it certainly illustrates the sense of proprietariness and protectiveness endemic in southern culture six decades later in Rockingham.

Townspeople and court watchers were less concerned with legalities and more focused on personal matters. Had Ormond debauched Elizabeth? Were they effectively married in the eyes of God, her reputation ruined? Or was she a virgin and he a dastardly liar, out for her money? Or maybe not right in his head after his war experiences?

From around the South, those most knowledgeable about legal wrangling predicted that any prosecution attacks on Miss Cole's character and chastity would help her father in the jury's eyes. Although melodramatic novels may mention the "unwritten law" or "the code of the South," did such an alternate to the rule of law exist? Or was it simply a romantic notion? Arguably, jurors in more recent times have applied other unwritten laws—

reluctant, for instance, to convict a woman of a crime because some juries feel protective or sympathetic with what they see as the gentler sex.

This case took place long before the law recognized stalking as an offense, so it is difficult to determine if what happened in Rockingham would fit our current definition. Jurors at the time, though, certainly understood the frustration of a father who felt that his daughter and his family were threatened by someone who kept ignoring his agreement to leave them alone, who persisted in pushing the boundaries. And today, how would a court handle a diagnosis of posttraumatic stress disorder following Ormond's service overseas?

Patriotism ran deep in the region. Jurors invariably knew other families whose loved ones had come home from the fighting impaired in some way. The victim's father had been a local minister, and the defendant was a wealthy man. The casting made for a story where loyalties shifted on the basis of more than just the facts and for which the outcome was uncertain.

The Associated Press reported on October 3, 1925, that when the jury came into the courtroom that morning, it came groomed for the day: "For forty minutes prior to the appearance they had monopolized one of Rockingham's barber shops, with Sheriff H.D. Baldwin standing guard at the door." Of course, the jury was all male.

The testimony at trial did not disappoint. In particular, reporters and townspeople hung on every word from Elizabeth Cole and her father, who testified in his own defense.

On October 12, just over two weeks after the court first convened, the jury acquitted William Cole of murder. It did not arrive at that verdict easily; the deliberations lasted twenty-one hours, spread over three days with three ballots taken. The first vote was eight to four to acquit. The second, at 7:30

Above: Side entrance to Richmond County Courthouse in Rockingham, site of the Ormond/Cole trial. *Photo by Cathy Pickens.*

Opposite, inset: Cornerstone of Richmond County Courthouse. *Photo by Cathy Pickens.*

p.m. on the second day, was eleven to one. The hold-out juror asked to be allowed to sleep on it. Jurors who later agreed to speak about their experience said they were a praying group of men, and that's what they did.

The next morning, the jury acquitted Cole. But he was not allowed to leave his jail cell just yet. Under the law, to be found not guilty by reason of insanity required showing the defendant was not currently insane. The judge had been careful to explain that requirement to the lawyers. The next day, satisfied by the affidavits provided by the defense, William Cole was released.

The jurors said the slander letter was a deciding factor for them. For lawyers analyzing the case, the sticking point is that slander does not merit a death penalty in North Carolina—or in any other state. But for the jurors, as well as for many in the community, the circumstances surrounding this letter, Ormond's continuing conduct and the unwritten law governing a father's right and obligation allowed the lines between law and morality to blur.

In the community, the verdict did not reconcile the opposing sides. In November, Reverend Ormond filed a civil suit against William Cole seeking $150,000 in damages for the wrongful death of his son. In June 1926, the parties settled for $15,000 (about $200,000 in 2020 dollars), with Cole also paying Ormond's costs of bringing the suit.

Soon after the trial, Helen Hayes played the starring role in *Coquette*, a popular stage play about a southern flirt determined to have her way. Mary Pickford, by that time a powerhouse actress and one of the first female producers in Hollywood, brought the story, based loosely on the case, to movie theaters. Pickford chose this as her first "talkie" film and played the lead based on Elizabeth Cole, winning one of the first Academy Awards.

Whichever side they supported, most in Rockingham likely felt the story needed no dramatic Broadway or Hollywood embellishments.

Bob Hines: Rockingham's Unsolved

Crime cases typically focus on the victim, the hunt for the perpetrator and the punishment meted out. Few crime cases follow the damage left in the wake of those crimes, to the families on either side—and few tell such a story as well as the granddaughter of a taxi driver killed in Richmond County in 1939, in her own search into the family mystery.

Bob Hines, age forty-four, survived World War I and returned home to Richmond County, where he lived with his wife and eight children. Few people in North Carolina, who mostly made their living on farms or in textile mills, had benefited from the wave of speculation and prosperity during the 1920s, so when the Great Depression hit, things weren't really much worse for them. They were used to growing and preserving their own food, making their own clothes and making do.

When money got tight for his family, Bob Hines made do by taking a taxi driving job. Going to town on a Saturday to get supplies or socialize was a big deal for rural folks, so on Saturday, October 7, 1939, Hines worked uptown Rockingham. He came home to pick up his eighteen-year-old daughter, Doris, to give her a lift to her Saturday job at the dime store. He would pick her up at the end of the day so they could come home for supper together, as was their custom.

On that Saturday, though, he didn't come to the dime store. The owner of the Rockingham Café hired another cab driver to take Doris home, where she found her mother already worried at the delay. Bob was never late, never out of his routine.

The family waited until early the next morning and then got a neighbor to carry son Robert into town to search. The family asked other cab drivers if they'd seen him. They talked to a patrolman, who encouraged Mrs. Hines to stay home, just in case Bob returned. She couldn't though. She went searching with Robert and a neighbor, Melvin.

Granddaughter and author Barbara Mozingo, recounting the story, said, "They found him. He was laying face up on the ground with his throat cut and a bullet in his chest, surrounded by onlookers and law enforcement." Mrs. Hines undoubtedly wished she could forget that tragic, up-close view of her husband. And she probably wished she could better understand how suspects could be arrested, bound over for trial and released, with the case never solved. The tragedy was in Technicolor and the solution a hazy, undefined gray.

Barbara Mozingo recalled happy memories of visiting her Grandmother Hines's house, where all the kin and cousins always gathered. But she also knew things had been tough after her grandfather's death. Her own mother quit school to work, and her grandmother went to work in the textile mill. If providing for a large family was difficult with a hardworking husband, it was really a struggle without him.

Years later, having heard the kinds of oft-told but ill-defined stories that circulate in any family, Barbara Mozingo found the newspaper clippings about her grandfather's murder. In black and white, written with a tell-all gossipiness of news reporting at the time, she learned he'd been found "Throat Cut from Ear to Ear and Also Bullet through Body." He'd been robbed of seventy dollars and left at the side of a dirt road but in view of passersby, who found him early Sunday morning, about two miles west of Rockingham. A knife with a four-inch blade, his own pistol with one shot fired, his fountain pen and wallet were scattered on the ground near his body.

His cab was found later, parked between the Mason fertilizer warehouse and the McLaurin ice plant in west Rockingham. The blood patterns suggested that Hines's neck had been cut while he was sitting at the steering wheel. Crime scene photos show blood on the door and running board of the car. He was shot after he was stabbed.

The case brought to mind another murder in Rockingham only three years earlier. Barbara Mozingo reported that John Moore, a World War I veteran like her grandfather, was found floating in Ledbetter's Pond. W.W. King, the same coroner called to her grandfather's scene, was also called to Moore's death. In that case, though, taxi driver Lawrence Spradley was convicted of the murder. Moore was carrying a lot of cash, the motive for the murder.

The case of Mozingo's grandfather's death was not so easily solved. What in later years would have been a ticket to solving the case was found on the steering wheel: "excellent" fingerprints in blood and a bloody handprint on the back seat. Neither matched Bob Hines. A fingerprint could have gotten on the wheel at any time, but a bloody print was an indictment of whoever had driven the car to the ice plant after the murder.

An intoxicated woman was arrested, claiming she knew something about the crime. When she sobered up, she didn't know anything.

The State Bureau of Investigation (SBI) sent two officers to Richmond County. All the taxi drivers in the area agreed to be fingerprinted to rule them out, although no one explained in the press why they might be suspected.

Five days after the murder, the *Rockingham Post-Dispatch* announced that three men and two women were being held in jail, but none of them matched the fingerprint. The headline said, "Possibly Be Released Friday." The fingerprint turned out to be useless, as fingerprints are when the finger they match cannot be found.

But then, four years later, witness Robert Porter "bobs" up, as the headline punned, with a detailed account of what happened in the death car. From the first announcement, though, the reports suggested the confession might not resolve the case after all. As the *Rockingham Post-Dispatch* reported on September 1, 1943, the case "may be on the verge of really being 'broken,' or it may prove to be a figment of a man whose mind may not have been completely well since he was five years old."

Robert Porter wove a colorful tale of murder, implicating two men and a woman, who were arrested and held on bonds of $10,000 for the men and $750 for the woman.

Porter's story said that he and another guy were drinking, got a ride with Hines, got some fish to cook later, picked up two more guys, kept drinking, went to buy more liquor and kept riding around; then, in some ill-defined argument, one of the men who'd joined them pulled Hines's head back and the other cut his throat.

They dumped Hines from his Ford taxi, drove down the road, worried that he might not be dead, drove back and shot him. At that point in Porter's story, a woman had joined them, earning her arrest as an accessory after the fact.

Local attorney Elsie Webb, later one of the cofounders of the North Carolina (later Rockingham) Motor Speedway, was hired by the Hines family as a private prosecutor. The Hines family could well be frustrated with how slowly the case had moved. How did the cash-strapped family afford an attorney? Or did others in the community, perhaps attorney Webb himself, offer assistance? Those details are lost in the record.

What isn't lost is that Robert Porter's story was suspect from the beginning. Four months after the arrest announcement, in January 1944, the headline said, "Doctor Reports on Robert Porter, Says Not Insane, but Expert Wants More Time to Study Porter Regarding Delusions." Despite reservations about his reliability, Porter's story agreed with details at the murder scene. Was that enough to put him in the cab?

Dr. Maurice H. Greenhill, associate professor of neuropsychiatry at Duke University's School of Medicine, declared him not insane, which meant Porter could stand trial in October 1944. However, the same psychiatrist raised questions about whether Porter was telling the truth. Even though Porter could stand trial because he knew the difference between right and wrong, maybe he couldn't tell the difference between fact and fancy. According to the doctor, "The suspicion…is aroused that he might be a hysterical psychopathic personality." He testified that Porter might suffer from "a condition called pseudologia phantastica," where a psychopath can lie, not know it's a lie and "firmly believe in it."

As recently as 2014, the medical literature reported a case of a patient who told outlandish stories of jumping out of a helicopter a mile in the air into a pool of alligators to save a friend. Often called pathological lying, the lies tend to be "quite dazzling or fantastical," with "imaginative fluency" that attracts listeners. Unlike lies told to avoid consequences, these fanciful tales often include elements of truth and are told to improve the teller's social standing.

Was Porter's story just an elaborately woven lie to make him sound important? If so, could he have gotten enough details about the scene from local gossip?

Recognizing how the doctor's testimony undermined the state's case, the prosecutor and judge agreed to a mistrial. Three defendants were released on bond, and in February 1944, the state agreed to pay Dr. Greenhill $225 for "a Turn-key Job" of evaluating Porter's mental reliability with an eye to a future trial.

In the official record, the case seems to evaporate at that point. In 1964, a twenty-fifth-anniversary news article noted that the unsolved case still haunts the SBI. Willard Gatling, one of the investigating SBI agents, said, "We concluded a woman was involved and rounded up many suspects as well as bootleggers." He also revealed he'd gone undercover as a prisoner in the Richmond County jail, trying to solve the case.

Robert Porter's account of the murder was detailed and fit the physical facts. He pointed out that, in all the driving about and drinking, Hines never drank. (And those paying for the liquor would tend to keep count of such a detail.) According to Barbara Mozingo, her grandfather never drank. Would Porter know that if he wasn't there? On the other side of the case, the bloody fingerprint matched none of those linked to Porter's story.

The case remains unsolved, one of many with tantalizing clues and plenty of small-town gossip but not enough evidence to bring to a jury. At the heart is a family made poorer not only by the loss of its hardworking patriarch but also by the unanswered questions.

SWAMP OUTLAWS

Robeson County

The story of North Carolina folk hero (or criminal) Henry Berry Lowry (or Lowrie) is shrouded in the misty romanticism and shadowy facts that should obscure any good folk hero story.

Much about Henry Berry is in dispute: the correct spelling of his name, his ethnic heritage, the size of his gang, the extent of his exploits and even what ultimately happened to him. But the obscurities are part of the fascination, as the many stories told about him share enough details to make the outline of his exploits plausible.

One of a dozen children, Henry Berry grew up in Robeson County in an area known as Scuffletown, the land of the Lumbee. Pembroke now sits within the boundaries of old Scuffletown.

Dr. Malinda Maynor Lowery, an associate professor of history at UNC–Chapel Hill, published *The Lumbee Indians: An American Struggle*, a unique look at this region from the perspective of a seasoned academic historian who is also Lumbee. Others have debated how to classify Henry Berry Lowry and his family: Members of the Tuscarora tribe? Mixed-race migrants from Tidewater Virginia plantation slaves and native peoples? As Lowery explained, race is less important to Lumbee than their relationships with their kin and with their homeplace.

Some history is obscured by lack of records, as well as by political maneuvers motivated by racial politics. In 1885, the Lumbee were first

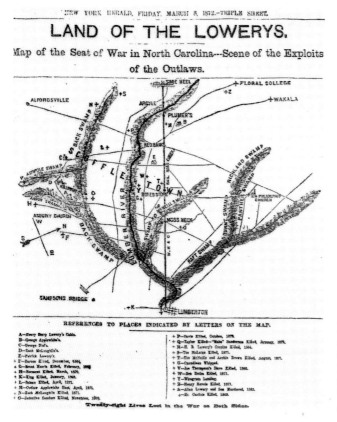

Map of Scuffletown, outside Lumberton, the area where Henry Berry Lowry grew up. *From the* New York Herald, *March 8, 1872.*

recognized as Croatan Indians by the state and then in the 1950s as the "Lumbee Indians of North Carolina," though without access to protection and support afforded federally recognized tribes. One historical account reported no record of Lowry or his colleagues ever identifying themselves as Indian, but several other accounts describe him as a "mixed blood Tuscarora." At least one newspaper asked if his "gang" were the "Black Ku Klux."

Henry Berry Lowry likely cared little for how he was classified by others. He was focused on taking care of his own. Most tellings of his tale start during the Civil War, when free people of color in the region were conscripted by the Confederate army to construct Fort Fisher, the world's largest dirt fortification at the time. The Cape Fear River provided important transport for people and supplies into the Wilmington area, and Fort Fisher successfully protected that route until the last months of the Civil War. Soldiers and slaves worked on building the fort; however, as stories tell, nearby plantation owners eventually balked at risking any more of their valuable slaves after a yellow fever outbreak and deaths due to starvation and harsh conditions. So, the Confederate army began conscripting residents in the region, many of them ancestors of the modern Lumbee, to do the hard, often deadly work.

Popular accounts say that Lowry's father and brother were killed when they failed to return after a leave from the fort. Soldiers hunted them down, "tried" them in a mock court and shot them. Stories say the teenage Henry Berry witnessed the killings from a hiding place and vowed vengeance. In Dr. Lowery's detailed account, the raids on local farms by General William T. Sherman's troops, conscription by the Confederates, rough justice practiced by the Home Guard left in charge of the region and simmering feuds among local families all paint a more complex backdrop for the legend.

Dr. Lowery poetically described the region where Henry Berry Lowry and the Lumbee have lived for generations: "Actually, 'land' is hardly the right term for this homeplace—it is water and soil, two perfect opposites flowing together since ancient times. Water knows nothing of difference or inferiority, though it may separate neighbors, towns, and nations."

The Lowry Gang was never large—maybe only twelve members at most—but it enjoyed support and protection from people in the area. The members never roamed far; their activities were confined to Robeson County. Like a swamp version of Robin Hood, Lowry took on the wealthy and politically powerful; his neighbors had no complaints with that.

He broke into businesses. He stole safes and blew them open. The popular favorite was the theft of the sheriff's safe, left open and empty in the middle of a road outside town, the $28,000 reportedly shared with those who'd been disadvantaged by elected officials and the elite. One story said the money was supposed to be the reward for the capture of Henry Berry Lowry.

The gang was charged with at least two murders—two men who had longstanding feuds with the Lowry family. One of those murder charges led to Lowry's arrest at his own wedding in 1865. The lawmen fell on him at the nuptials and hauled him off to Wilmington. Lowry escaped and returned to his new wife. Such is the stuff of legends.

The gang hampered train travel, the main mode of transportation for people and goods in the region. Several stories circulated about Lowry riding trains with or marching alongside soldiers out hunting for him, without being recognized. His supporters took delight in his ability to move among those who wanted to capture him yet were oblivious to his taunting. But he never robbed a train carrying the mail. During this period of Reconstruction following the Civil War, federal officials had a strong presence in the area, and Lowry knew not to rile them up.

Although Lowry and his gang never ventured far, his story traveled widely in the national press. Local business and political leaders tried to get the state or national authorities to intervene, but they declined. After all, the federal government had other things to worry about in the aftermath of the war, and from a distance, Lowry seemed like a contained problem. In Robeson County, though, he seemed powerful and undefeatable.

The State of North Carolina outlawed the gang in 1868, an unusual response to criminal activity. In 1872, the *New York Herald* sent George Alfred Townsend south to the Lumber River area to get the story on the "Lowry War." He found the region much as it remains today: humid and flat and full of pine trees. Turpentine and pine pitch were principal cash products. Most people grew vegetables and raised animals for meat or eggs. Townsend knew Lumberton to be the "stamping ground" of Lowry and that he'd never killed anyone outside of Robeson County. Townsend quoted the "Fighting Parson" Sinclair, who described Lowry as "one of those remarkable executive spirits that arises now and then in a raw community....He has passions but no weaknesses and his eye is on every point at once."

Even among his contemporaries, Lowry had mythical status. Those who encountered him described him as unfailingly polite, even when he ordered a white woman to cook him and his men a meal in her kitchen. He made her taste each dish, to make sure it wasn't poisoned, but also complimented her cooking, thanked her repeatedly and asked her to "get word to him" should she ever need his services.

In 1871, getting desperate to corral Lowry, the Police Guard captured the gang members' wives and held them hostage in the local jail. Lowry and his compatriots sent a letter spelling out their terms: release their wives or "the bloodiest times will be here than ever was before—the life of every man will be in jeopardy." The Police Guard released the women.

Lowry remained colorful and enigmatic to the end. In 1872, the gang robbed $20,000 of goods from a store in Lumberton and took the store's safe and its $20,000. After that hefty haul, Lowry disappeared. Some said, on good authority, that he died in a gun-cleaning accident in the woods near his home and his body was secretly buried. A few said the accidental shooting was a ruse. Others said he left the area, that he was "loaded right here at Moss Neck" or "he was shipped off in a large box." The stories are equally divided on the outcome and equally insistent on the infallibility of sources.

What happened to him remains a mystery. The only certainty is that the $12,000 bounty on his head, dead or alive, was never collected. In 1872, that would equal a 2020 purchasing power of more than $200,000.

Starting in 1976, *Strike at the Wind!*, an outdoor play recounting the life of Henry Berry Lowry, was performed for twenty years and has enjoyed periodic revivals at UNC–Pembroke.

In 2000, award-winning novelist Josephine Humphreys, from South Carolina's swampy coastline, wrote *Nowhere Else on Earth*, her vision of the life of Rhoda Strong, Lowry's wife. In a 2002 interview with *Charlotte Observer* reporter Elizabeth Leland, local historian Bruce Barton said, "To me, she is the most interesting character out of that period because she kept secrets. I think she loved Henry Berry Lowrie so much that she gave him up." From his disappearance in 1872 to her death in 1909, she never told anyone what happened to him. Barton said, "I think she knew where he was at."

UNPRECEDENTED

The story had to grab headlines from the start, even before the twists. The brutal stabbing murder of a young mother and her two little daughters in what should have been their safe suburban home. The baby sister left alive, crying in her crib, so dehydrated that a doctor said she couldn't have lived much longer had a neighbor not noticed three days of newspapers stacking up in front of the house. The heartbroken father, a man whose life and work involved protecting and defending others, out of town and not there to protect his family when they needed him.

First the tragedy, then the twists. Police and prosecutors put in the hard work of identifying the perpetrator, gathering the evidence, convincing a jury and winning a death penalty verdict, only to have the North Carolina Supreme Court overturn the conviction because the prosecutor had been too zealous, too graphic in showing the jury what happened.

The defendant was released. He got a second trial. Then he got a third.

The May 1985 murder in Fayetteville could have happened in any small town or suburb or city. Brutal, senseless crimes do occur. Women and children are victims. Fayetteville law enforcement officers routinely saw more than their share of violent death; after all, the city was full of young men stationed at the military bases, many away from home for the first time and hanging out in bars and other places where trouble can find them or they can start it.

Summerhill Road sign, across the street from the Eastburns' house. *Courtesy of Cathy Pickens.*

But as inured as they were to violence, the officers couldn't have expected the scene they found at the Eastburn house. As horrifying as the crime scene in the brick ranch on Summerhill Road was, as devastating for the husband and father, Gary Eastburn, it also became a crime that wouldn't end. Setting a legal or forensic precedent is interesting to those who study such things, removed from the reality of loss. But no one would want to experience what prompted the interesting precedents in this case.

U.S. Air Force captain Gary Eastburn, head of air traffic control at Pope Air Force Base, was attending Squadron Officer School in Alabama, preparing for a transfer to England. He hated to be away from his young family but was glad they would join him on his assignment overseas.

He and Katie looked forward to their regular Saturday morning phone calls. On the Saturday before Mother's Day, he tried repeatedly and then called his neighbor, Bob Seefeldt, asking him to check on them. Seefeldt knocked but got no answer. The family car was parked in the driveway.

The next morning, Mother's Day, May 12, 1985, Seefeldt noticed three newspapers on the driveway next door; the car still had not been moved. He again rang the doorbell. Again, no one answered. This time, though, he heard what sounded like the baby crying inside. He called law enforcement.

Through the window, the responding sheriff's deputy saw the baby, not quite two-year-old Jana, crying in her crib. He cut the screen and climbed in the window to reach her. The strong, unmistakable odor of death confirmed his fear. From the hallway, he could see bodies. He handed the baby out the window to safety, radioed for help and climbed back out the window.

The responding detectives, Robert Bittle and Jack Watts, arrived at about 1:00 p.m. on Mother's Day. They knew the scene was a bad one. What they didn't know was how long they would continue to live with this case.

In 2011, Nicholas Schmidle covered the case in depth for the *New Yorker*. Detective Bittle told him, "Death has a smell, its own aroma. I'll never forget the smell in there." Or the sights. The first hint of what happened were jeans, two loose buttons and torn panties in the living room. In a bedroom, Kara, age five, was hidden under her Star Wars blanket, stabbed, her throat cut. In the master bedroom, Erin, age three, had similar knife wounds. Their mother, Katie, was on the other side of the bed, partially naked, stabbed fifteen times, her throat cut as well. All had been dead for a while. Judging from the newspapers out front and last known sightings, they'd probably died sometime Thursday night or Friday morning.

Detective Watts called Gary Eastburn in Alabama, giving him news the father must have already feared. As soon as Captain Eastburn flew to Fayetteville, he went straight to the sheriff's office. His alibi was solid. The detectives asked what else had been happening in the family. For a few months, since he'd left for training, Katie and their babysitter had been getting what she considered threatening, anonymous phone calls from someone who called her "Mrs. Eastburn." In 1985, landline phone numbers, names and addresses were easily available from printed phone books, so the caller would know her name. Did he know her, though? Tracing the last call received by dialing *69 wasn't an option then.

Anticipating the family's move to England, Katie had placed a classified ad in a military community newspaper offering their English setter for sale. Fearing that Dixie wouldn't survive the international quarantine, Katie wanted their pet to find a good home, but she also wanted to keep the "cranks" away, so she listed an asking price of ten dollars.

On Wednesday, May 15, in a home on the other side of Fayetteville, the Hennises, another military couple, were watching the television news while eating lunch. The newscaster said detectives wanted to talk to a man driving a white Chevette who'd picked up a dog on Summerhill Road on Tuesday, a week earlier. Tim Hennis and his wife, Angela, knew Tim was that man, so they drove with their baby daughter to the Law Enforcement Center, where Tim told detectives about the dog.

A tall, blond, athletic army sergeant, Hennis did the detailed work of supervising the packing of parachutes. He had called about the dog and driven to meet Katie at the Eastburn house on Tuesday, May 7. He was confident enough to bring a leash to take the dog home, to see whether it got along with a little spitz he and his wife already owned. He loaded the setter into his white Chevette and drove away. That's all he knew.

That might have ended that line of inquiry, except another witness had come forward, after he saw ambulances outside the Eastburn home on Mother's Day. He'd seen a man leaving the Eastburns at about 3:30 a.m. on Friday.

The witness, Patrick Cone, came forward reluctantly, finally contacting investigators about midnight on Monday. He was African American, had some run-ins with the law and had a job he didn't want to endanger. But he'd told family and co-workers about an odd exchange with a big white guy in the middle of the night as he left his girlfriend's house—it had been unusual enough to comment on. Cone's family warned him not to get involved—that it wasn't any of his business. But the story about what had happened to Katie and her daughters bothered him, so he called the sheriff's office.

Later, defense attorneys would take issue with Patrick Cone, his reliability, the consistency of his testimony and even his description of the night as "clear." But from the beginning, Cone described a very tall white man wearing jeans, a knit cap and a Members Only black jacket, carrying a garbage bag over his shoulder. The two men were close enough that the towering man spoke to him—something about getting an early start this morning. Cone walked on down Summerhill Road and then looked back to see the taillights of a white Chevette driving off.

A police sketch artist, in a quick rendering from Cone's description, created a rough drawing of a man with a mustache, a long face, sleepy eyes and thin blond hair.

Interestingly, when the case eventually reached the North Carolina Supreme Court, the majority opinion wrote of the "tenuousness of this identification" and that Cone revised his "impression of the stature and build of the man." However, in his dissent, Justice Burney Mitchell wrote that he didn't "find the State's evidence nearly so weak nor the eyewitness identification testimony nearly so 'tenuous' as does the majority." The detectives said, from his first report, that Patrick Cone consistently described the "big white guy" he'd seen outside the Eastburn house in the wee hours of Friday morning. He told co-workers he'd seen "one big white dude." He described the trash bag and the knit cap and the white Chevette.

For Detective Watts, Cone was not only consistent but also accurate. When Hennis came to the station about his dog-buying visit, the detective was struck by how much the man sitting in front of him looked like the sketch they'd just seen: the blond hair, the long face, the thin mustache.

Tim Hennis answered questions for seven hours that first meeting. Watts recognized that Hennis was sharper than most; he would learn Hennis's score on the army's general aptitude test was extremely high. Later, when musing on why Hennis agreed to come in and answer questions for so long, the consensus was he wanted to know what the investigators knew—and he thought he was smarter than they were.

Hennis agreed to be photographed and provided hair and blood samples. Detective Watts took the photograph, added five other blond guys with mustaches to a photo lineup and asked Cone if he recognized anybody. Cone picked photo no. 2: Hennis.

That night, warrant in hand, sheriff's investigators and SBI agents knocked on Hennis's door. "I hope you guys know what you're doing," Hennis said as they arrested him. Hennis's father was a retired IBM executive. He wasted no time hiring Gerald Beaver and Billy Richardson, two high-profile Fayetteville criminal defense lawyers. Throughout, Hennis's family supported him, putting up all their financial resources, convinced that investigators had made a rush-to-judgment mistake.

Gathering the Evidence

If past violence is the best predictor of future violence, none of Hennis's brushes with the law would seem to presage such a vicious attack. Stemming from his poor money management, he had bad check charges almost everywhere he'd ever lived and had even lost his flight school slot for lying about them. Investigators learned he'd recently had a physical confrontation with a co-worker at Bennigan's restaurant, where he worked a second job. Not exactly a long rap sheet, but not exactly squeaky clean either.

The state's evidence started with Patrick Cone's photo lineup pick, his description of the clothing, the police sketch and his linking a car similar to Hennis's to the street in front of the Eastburns' house around the time of the murder. In addition, by Hennis's own testimony, he'd met Katie Eastburn on Tuesday, although he said he never saw her again.

The state also found that Hennis had taken his black Members Only jacket to a dry cleaner the day after the murder. As defense evidence would point out, no blood was found on the jacket and dry cleaning fluid wouldn't eradicate all traces of blood.

Neighbors reported that Hennis tended an hours-long blazing bonfire in a metal drum in his backyard on the Saturday after the murder, something he'd never done before. Hennis said he was burning papers and military manuals because his wife had given him the ultimatum to clean his mess out of the second bedroom while she was out of town visiting family.

Missing from the Eastburn house after the murder were only a few items: some cash, an ATM card and the paper with the ATM password. The card had been used twice in the two days after the murder, both times to withdraw $150, the maximum amount allowed. Coincidentally, Tim Hennis paid $300 he owed in late rent the next week.

Interviewing others who had ATM transactions around the times the missing card was used, police found a woman who'd seen a tall blond man in a light-color car on Saturday morning.

Two witnesses had now placed Tim Hennis in compromising places. In rebuttal, the defense hired Dr. Elizabeth Loftus, renowned for research proving the unreliability of eyewitness testimony and for the effectiveness of her courtroom testimony. She was able to show the weaknesses in Patrick Cone's identification of the man outside the Eastburn house. As Dr. Loftus pointed out, when Cone was shown the photo lineup, Hennis was the only one pictured wearing a Members Only jacket. The witness who said she'd seen Hennis at the ATM when the Eastburns' card was used came forward only after his photo appeared in news reports. Those situations can skew what witnesses think they saw.

Motive was also a question. Hennis was behind on his rent, but was money the motive? Or did one of Hennis's former girlfriends provide a more plausible motive? He'd dated Nancy Maeser for a while. On Thursday, May 9, he stopped by her house while his wife was out of town. Her husband was stationed in Germany. He might have expected some "old friend" benefits; she sidestepped that by touching his wedding ring and asking about his marriage. He told her his wife had left him; his wife later testified she had just gone to visit her parents.

The state's theory was that after getting rejected, he remembered another attractive young woman whose husband was out of town. Maybe Katie Eastburn would be interested in a visit. What prompted the attacks on the family and in exactly which order they occurred, only the killer would know. And he wasn't talking.

The First Trial

A little more than a year after the murders, in the summer of 1986, the case went to trial with William VanStory as lead prosecutor.

As an enlisted man, Hennis could have been tried in a military court. With Congressional adoption of the Uniform Code of Military Justice in 1950, courts-martial had jurisdiction over crimes committed by military

Sculpture garden commemorating the armed services at N.C. Veterans Park in Fayetteville. *Photo by Cathy Pickens.*

personnel both on and off base. To maintain discipline and control, the military needed to punish service members who harmed civilians.

In practice, most crimes off-base were handled by the Cumberland County district attorney. One exception to that practice haunted the Eastburn investigation from the beginning: the specter of Green Beret Dr. Jeffrey MacDonald and the 1970 murders of his wife and two daughters.

Dr. MacDonald was the only survivor of the attacks on his family in their base housing. Only six months before his family was attacked, the 1969 Manson family murders in Los Angeles made news. MacDonald claimed that drug-crazed hippies also attacked him and his family, which fueled conspiracy theories and armchair detectives from the early days of the investigation.

Family members, particularly his former father-in-law, at first stood by MacDonald but later became convinced of his guilt. Joe McGinniss, the writer to whom MacDonald granted access during his trial preparation, became convinced of his guilt too, prompting the best-selling book *Fatal Vision*.

Because the murders occurred in on-base housing, the military investigated and took over the prosecution, charging MacDonald with murder. But in the military version of a preliminary hearing, the charges were dismissed. MacDonald resumed his civilian life.

Had MacDonald's father-in-law not pushed for more investigation, the doctor may have lived out his new California lifestyle without encumbrance. But in 1979, civilian authorities in Fayetteville decided to prosecute him in federal court. He was convicted and sentenced to life. The trial occurred only six years before the Eastburn murders, so the saga was fresh in Fayetteville's memory.

MacDonald's case stayed in the news for decades because of his willingness to talk on television and his continued push to reopen his case. From the early days after the Eastburn case, echoes of the MacDonald murders were heard in the community. In a weird side note, the Eastburns' babysitter, a high school student, was enamored of the charming doctor after writing a school book report on *Fatal Vision*. She corresponded with him in prison and became convinced of his innocence. Investigators had to wonder in the early days: was there a connection? They dreaded the press linking the cases and even wondered if somehow MacDonald could have orchestrated the deaths to prove the killer was still out there, to throw his conviction into doubt.

Some speculated the military still felt stung by criticism of its handling of the MacDonald case. Or maybe it just made sense for murders off-base to be handled in the state court, which had more experience with murder trials.

In any event, lead prosecutor William VanStory was ready. He wanted the jury to have a sense of outrage at the brutality of the murders, at a little baby left to dehydrate and almost die and the loss of a beautiful, loving family. On a specially installed giant screen, more than three by five feet, VanStory projected graphic photos from the crime scene and the autopsies. In addition, he passed eight-by-ten mostly color copies of the same photos to the jury for them to study. Of the ninety-nine crime scene and autopsy photos available, he showed only one-third of them, but the prosecutor took his time. He wanted the jury to know what had happened, in all its horror.

The first jury vote was nine to three for guilt. After deliberations, the jury found Tim Hennis guilty of rape and of three murders. He was sent to Death Row. Post-trial photos show Hennis offering a brave smile of encouragement to his wife as he towered over the officer leading him in handcuffs to Central Prison in Raleigh.

The Appeal

Death penalty cases are routinely appealed. They are not routinely overturned, especially in North Carolina. The Hennis appeal, though, set a precedent still cited in North Carolina murder trials. Rule 403 of the state's Rules of Evidence reads:

> *Exclusion of relevant evidence on grounds of prejudice, confusion, or waste of time.*
>
> *Although relevant, evidence may be excluded if its probative value is substantially outweighed by the danger of unfair prejudice, confusion of the issues, or misleading the jury, or by considerations of undue delay, waste of time, or needless presentation of cumulative evidence. (1983, c. 701, s. 1.)*

In other words, sometimes valid, accurate evidence may be excluded because it is *too* good, too descriptive, too accurate or too gruesome, to the point that jurors can't carefully weigh how important the evidence is because they can't forget how lurid it is.

Where is the line drawn between making the crime and the pain real to those who haven't seen or suffered it and creating impressions so gruesome that jurors are unfairly prejudiced? The line drawing is left to the discretion of the judge, but that line isn't easy to draw.

The size of the sixteen-square-foot display screen, the fact that it hung over Hennis's head so jurors couldn't help but see him as they watched the horrific photographs, the repetition of the photographs—all served to sear the images of decaying, bloody corpses of small girls and their mother into the minds of the jury.

The appellate court decided that prosecutors had crossed the line in this case. The court held the large screen hanging behind Hennis "quite probably enhanced the prejudicial impact of the slides." Even though the prosecutor had reduced the number of images used, they were repetitive. Some were presented in silence, perhaps adding to their effect. The court held that the prejudicial effect outweighed the value of showing the photos.

Tim Hennis won a new trial. In his 1989 retrial, his lawyers already knew what the state would bring and invested hours in unearthing evidence to undermine it. One mysterious missing witness prompted their drive to "find the walker." A man lived in the Eastburns' neighborhood and walked the streets late at night wearing a jacket and beanie hat and carrying a backpack over one shoulder, but no one had found him for the first trial. For the second

New Hanover County Courthouse in Wilmington, site of Tim Hennis's second trial and acquittal. *Courtesy of North Carolina Judicial Branch.*

trial, the defense did "find the walker." He'd been away attending Appalachian State. And he looked remarkably like Tim Hennis, enough to be his brother.

The defense team also investigated the story of a woman living down the street who'd been terrorized by phone calls from an apparent stalker. Was this the same person who'd called the Eastburn house and unnerved Katie and the babysitter? Could that be another suspect?

A defense expert also rebutted testimony that dry cleaning would have eradicated any blood on the Members Only jacket—regular dry cleaning wouldn't remove blood, the expert said.

The defense team knew the opposing side's case and was prepared. This time, Tim Hennis was not led away in handcuffs. In 1989, Hennis left the courtroom a free man, one of the few to ever walk free from Death Row.

Tim's wife and the Hennis family, who'd never wavered in their support, were ecstatic. Hennis reenlisted in the army. He received more than three years' back pay for his time spent in prison. His first duty assignment was, ironically, as a prison guard at Fort Knox. He did tours in the first Gulf War and in Somalia. He retired in 2004 to Lakewood, Washington, with his family.

The Eastburn family and friends, and the prosecutors and investigators, knew that the murderer of Katie, Kara and Erin was still out there.

New Evidence

In 1985, at the time of the murders, forensic use of DNA was fledgling at best. The first crime-solving use of DNA wasn't until the following year, in England, when biologist Alec Jeffreys was asked to determine whether DNA evidence supported the confession of a young man to two rape-murders. It didn't. He hadn't committed those crimes. Rather than convicting a criminal, DNA was first used to free an innocent man.

The police in Fayetteville weren't rubes. They kept up with what was going on and knew about the British case. But Scotland Yard hadn't agreed to help when contacted by investigators about the Eastburn case. The first U.S. DNA case came the year after the Hennis trial, in 1987—a rape conviction.

Technology at the time of the first and second trials had advanced from testing for simple blood type to measuring PGM genetic markers. In rape cases, though, the blood type of the victim could "mask" the PGM markers in the semen. At the second trial, an FBI expert explained that the time lapse between the murder and the discovery could have aided the masking. In addition, separating multiple DNA donors was a challenge—until the technology improved.

Steady improvements in forensic DNA testing changed everything in the case. Years later, still searching for the killer, investigators submitted semen to the SBI lab. A match came back: Tim Hennis. The link was astonishingly certain: "1.2 quadrillion times more likely to be from Hennis than any other white person in North Carolina," reported the *New Yorker* in 2011.

The district attorney had his killer.

And he could do nothing about it.

The framers of the U.S. Constitution, seeking to protect citizens from the abuses of government, said no one could be tried twice for the same crime. Buried in a list of other protections provided by the Fifth Amendment (including the right not to be compelled to be a witness against yourself in a criminal case, often referred to as "taking the Fifth") are these words: "…nor shall any person be subject for the same offence to be twice put in jeopardy of life or limb."

The State of North Carolina had already put Tim Hennis in jeopardy of life or limb for the state offenses of rape and triple murder. The state Supreme Court had granted him a new trial because the first trial had errors. The state had failed to convict him at the second trial. He walked free. Now the state couldn't get another bite at the apple, couldn't go for best two out of three. Tim Hennis was a free man, protected by the double jeopardy clause in the Fifth Amendment.

Or was he? The Constitution protected against prosecution for the *same* offense. That offense was violation of the state homicide and rape statutes. It didn't protect against prosecution by another sovereign for crimes under its statutes. And at the time of the murders, Hennis was an enlisted man, subject to the military's laws.

District Attorney Edward Grannis presented the new DNA evidence to Fort Bragg attorneys. They did what they had the power to do: Hennis was ordered to reenlist (for which he received pay and benefits) and retried in a court-martial for the three murders. The court-martial was held twenty-one years after North Carolina acquitted Hennis in his second trial. Little baby Jana, who hadn't been old enough to remember that night, was now twenty-six years old.

The defense predictably attacked the handling of evidence and introduced one new claim never made in the earlier trials: yes, his DNA was present; yes, they'd had sex, but it was consensual. That defense argument didn't persuade a jury of military men often deployed, leaving their own wives home alone. In April 2010, they deliberated for three hours before finding him guilty. In a 106-page opinion, the Army Court of Criminal Appeals analyzed the case and upheld his conviction.

In 2020, Hennis sat with three other men on military Death Row at Fort Leavenworth, Kansas: Hasan Akbar, who killed sixteen fellow soldiers in a 2003 grenade attack in Kuwait; Nidal Hasan, an army psychiatrist who shot and killed thirteen at Fort Hood, Texas, to aid Islamic insurgents in 2009; and Ronald Gray, another Fort Bragg solider convicted of three rapes, murders and an attempted murder in 1988.

In three separate, hard-fought trials, the evidence was thoroughly vetted and yet left questions: Patrick Cone, the witness who didn't want to come forward and who was, as his family predicted, criticized for getting involved; the Members Only jacket with no blood on it; the precise parachute repair work he did for the military; the crime scene with no blood, hair, footprints or fingerprints that could be matched to Hennis; the signs of cleaning and the garbage bag thrown over the shoulder of a man seen leaving the driveway; the accused's supportive wife and family; his money troubles and his late rent payment; his burn barrel; his marital infidelities; and his lack of a history of violence, especially sexual violence. Add to that the atmosphere of Fayetteville in the short years since the Jeffrey MacDonald trial: the babysitter pen pal; hand-scrawled letters to Hennis in prison and to the sheriff, signed "Mr. X," claiming responsibility for the murders; and the never-solved harassing phone calls to women in the neighborhood. Then the legal debate over double jeopardy and the extension of military justice into crimes off-base. The large, glowering man whose attorneys worried about how jurors would perceive him, whose little girl banged on the prison partition yelling for her daddy to "open it!" The man who became one of the poster children for wrongful conviction, the man rescued from Death Row by diligent defense lawyers.

Then the DNA. And the questions that followed: How could we not have seen it? Did we still get it wrong? What if…?

ONLINE SWINGERS
AND A SHOOTER

Cumberland County

U.S. military base towns have their own distinct demographics: Large, often transient populations, from every socioeconomic, ethnic and geographical background. Young people away from home for the first time or untethered by families. Young families away from the support of parents and friends, building new relationships but knowing they aren't there to stay. Wild parts of town catering to military paydays with massage parlors, gambling, bars and prostitution.

In North Carolina, the defense sector is the second-largest employer in the state, representing the U.S. Army (Fort Bragg in Fayetteville, including the former Pope Air Force Base, by population the largest military installation in the world), the U.S. Air Force (Seymour Johnson Air Force Base in Goldsboro), the U.S. Marines Corps (Camp Lejeune in Jacksonville, including a Naval Command), the U.S. Coast Guard (Support Unit Elizabeth City) and countless support industries.

Fayetteville has not always enjoyed the best reputation, with nicknames like Vietnam War–era "Fayettenam," "Fayette-hell" and the thickly drawled "Fedvul." But it's also been named the most patriotic city in the United States, a city proud to say that "when the President calls 911, the phone rings at Fort Bragg."

The warrior culture, a strong sense of duty, a family history of military service and a desire to travel and learn skills valuable in the private sector—all

"One hundred bronze hands, raised to shoulder height…to recite the Oath of Service." Life-size casts from veterans of every North Carolina county, N.C. Veterans Park, Fayetteville. *Photo by Cathy Pickens.*

are attractions to a military career. U.S. Air Force captain Martin Theer and his high school sweetheart and wife, Michelle, were "military brats." Marty attended the Air Force Academy. Michelle joined the Reserves and then pursued her college degree and her doctorate in psychology while she followed Marty to assignments in Florida and Fayetteville.

Fayetteville hadn't been Michelle's first choice—not as dynamic as where they'd grown up in Colorado or lived in Florida. But she quickly found work with Dr. Thomas Harbin's psychology practice while she worked toward her North Carolina certification.

Fayetteville didn't really need another murder case that attracted national attention, but it got one in December 2000. Just a few days before Christmas, handsome, decorated air force pilot Captain Marty Theer was shot to death in the parking lot of his wife's psychology practice. What followed were years of rumors, investigations, a court-martial, a fugitive search and another much-watched murder trial.

As with lots of military marriages, the distance from extended family and the loss of their close support, the erratic travel and periods of deployment,

English Saddle Drive in Fayetteville, in the neighborhood where Michelle and Marty Theer lived. *Photo by Cathy Pickens.*

the single-minded focus on building a military career and the loneliness of an uprooted spouse took a toll on the Theers' storybook marriage. They were a handsome couple; Marty loved Michelle but was also devoted to his job. She had a career and wasn't sure about his push for children. The move to Fayetteville meant separating Michelle from a network she'd developed while finishing her education. Lots of young couples face those pressures and questions.

Although the murder scene itself was straightforward, what led up to it and exactly how it happened continues to invite speculation. As with any murder case, the story changes based on perspective, on loyalties, on what can be corroborated and what is purely self-serving.

On December 17, 2000, three couples associated with Harbin & Associates drove a little over an hour to Cary for an office dinner to celebrate the holiday season. Afterward, Marty and Michelle Theer drove one of the couples back to the Harbin office parking lot about 10:30 p.m. to pick up their car. The Theers left for home, stopped for gas and then returned to the office because Michelle had forgotten a book she needed to finish a report the next day.

She said she climbed the external metal stairs at the back of the building, closer to her second-floor office than the front door. She was inside for a few minutes when she heard the popping sounds of gunfire outside. When she got the nerve to peek out the door, she saw Marty lying at the bottom of the stairs. She thought he was still breathing as she cradled his head. She'd rushed down the steps, accidentally locking herself out without her keys. She ran a block or two to where lights shone inside a video rental store and got a clerk to call 911.

The police took photos, questioned her, started building a time line and called in a tracking dog. The dog picked up a scent in the shrubs lining the parking lot, a few feet from where the body lay. Michelle said she might have seen some movement there. The dog tracked around the building and across

Stairwell where Marty Theer was shot; the back entrance to Michelle Theer's office is at top of stairs. *Photo by Cathy Pickens.*

Raeford Road toward the Highland Country Club and its golf course before losing the scent. The dog couldn't know if that scent had anything to do with the shooting, and the scent never led to a suspect, only to the suggestion that someone else was there and ran away, perhaps leaving the area in a car. A defense attorney later would question the skills and experience of the dog.

At first, police suspected a robbery, although a business office parking lot at night was an odd location for a robber and Theer's keys and wallet were still in his pockets.

The autopsy suggested a shooter with better-than-average skills. Theer had been hit five times: twice in the chest and twice in the legs from behind. The trajectory and blood on the stairs said the shots came from below, as Theer was climbing the stairs toward the exterior metal door. One shot shattered a leg bone. For the final shot to the head, Theer was on the ground at the bottom of the stairs. The shooter stood close to deliver that last shot just behind his left ear.

When an air force captain is shot in a nice part of town after a Christmas party, the press will be interested and the investigation will move with speed and purpose. Tips came in. Police learned the Theer marriage had hit some bumps. Routine searches into phone records and computers began to reveal the interesting ways Michelle kept herself entertained while her husband worked and traveled. Michelle had at least one boyfriend, maybe more.

Although it was in the early days of computer forensics, Officer C.T. Williams with the Fayetteville Police Department had developed the skills. He spent hours locating and rebuilding erased files. The search would take years to complete. He couldn't recover everything, but it was enough to find Michelle's online searches for men interested in casual sex, e-mail conversations indicating she'd made more than one connection, online and in person, and one man with whom she had an intimate relationship.

Solicitation online for casual sex, swingers clubs where sexual partners were exchanged, the breakdown of a handsome, successful couple's marriage and stories of a love triangle would attract readers. The story only got more intriguing—and more tragic.

U.S. Army staff sergeant John Diamond met Michelle in a Yahoo! chat room. Their affair was well documented in computer and phone exchanges and by her vigilant neighbors noting his teal Pontiac Firebird parked down the street from her house, often overnight. When questioned, Diamond admitted to the affair but knew nothing about Theer's murder.

A friend of Diamond's came forward with an important lead: Diamond had borrowed a Smith & Wesson 5906 semiautomatic pistol a few days

Property of
The Bureau of Alcohol, Tobacco, Firearms and Explosives

Smith & Wesson 5906, the model of handgun used in the Theer murder. *Courtesy of the Bureau of Alcohol, Tobacco, Firearms and Explosives.*

before the shooting, a gun he'd borrowed before for practice at a private range. That pistol was one of only two models that could have fired the shell casings recovered at the scene.

With police taping the conversation, the friend called Diamond and asked for his pistol back, saying police wanted to test it. Diamond explained his car window had been smashed while he was out of town and the gun stolen from under the front seat. That tape gave investigators an opening. Because his car was parked on base at the time of the theft and because having private weapons on base was illegal, Diamond was arrested.

Investigators got permission from the homeowner across the street to set up video surveillance of Michelle's house and driveway. The video caught an unexpected piece of evidence that became important only after listening to Diamond's taped conversation about the theft. Soon after the time Diamond said his window was smashed and the gun stolen, he appeared on video pulling up to Michelle's house. The surveillance camera clearly showed the window glass was intact. Diamond had the kind of gun that killed Theer and had lied about how that gun went missing.

In 2000, investigators were in the early stages of unlocking the growing potential of cellphones to track and record activities, but in this case, one of their most important initial finds was something they couldn't have found in cell records. Michelle volunteered that she'd excused herself for a restroom break at the restaurant in Cary and called John Diamond. She said the call was innocuous—she wanted advice about repairs to her yellow Corvette, but when he didn't answer, she hung up without talking to him.

An unanswered call wouldn't have registered on her phone records. But her mention of the call gave investigators another important piece of a puzzle they were putting together. They suspected the call signaled Diamond that the Theers were leaving the Raleigh restaurant. They suspected that Diamond knew where to station himself to surprise Theer while Michelle was in her office picking up a book.

Diamond and his wife, Lourdes, had an on-again, off-again relationship. At first, she said he was home with her watching the movie *The Patriot* on television all evening. Later, as the case uncovered things she didn't know about the husband she loved, Lourdes changed her story. She said Diamond got a phone call at about 9:00 p.m., put on his winter coat and left the house.

Fayetteville detective Ralph Clinkscales, who led the investigation, believed that Michelle had set up Marty Theer. Without that phone call, he said, Diamond wouldn't have known Marty's movements that night.

Diamond's initial arrest was for the military code gun violation. Military and civilian investigators then worked together to build the case in the Theer homicide. In August 2001, Diamond was tried before a six-member military tribunal of four officers and two enlisted men. A verdict would require only four votes.

Michelle refused to answer questions on the stand, pleading her Fifth Amendment Constitutional protections. Diamond was found guilty and sentenced to life in a military prison. Michelle had not yet been charged, but that didn't mean she wasn't under investigation. For her part, she wasn't sitting idle. As investigators later discovered, she was working to disappear into a new identity. As soon as the indictment against her was handed down on May 21, she was gone—for four months.

Thanks to a slip-up by a new man in her life, she was finally tracked to Florida. Michelle's new boyfriend called Michelle's father from his mother's home phone in Nebraska rather than using a burner phone with a random number, as Michelle had instructed. Police quickly picked up the trail by following the new boyfriend.

In culling through what she'd left behind in New Orleans during her run, investigators knew she'd studied books on changing her identity. When they found her, she was operating under two aliases: Lisa Pendragon and Alexandra Solomon. They arrested her at her Lauderdale-by-the-Sea

Cumberland County Courthouse in Fayetteville, site of Michelle Theer's 2004 trial. *Courtesy of North Carolina Judicial Branch.*

apartment the same day she had a chemical peel to clear acne scars from her face, to supplement plastic surgery to straighten her nose and tighten her eyelids, among other work. Was she making herself look better, with her hair dyed blonde and thousands of dollars in cosmetic surgery? Or was she making herself look different so she could change her identity a few more times and be gone for good? She was arrested in Florida on August 5, 2002.

At her trial and on appeal, her attorneys tried to introduce evidence that Marty had also strayed from their marriage. They also tried to keep out evidence about Marty's $500,000 life insurance and her interest in his pending bonus, her Wiccan beliefs and, in particular, the eight boxes containing twenty-one thousand documents taken from her computer records that made her appear a "moral degenerate" and which revealed her eBay search for "body bag disaster pouches."

The Fayetteville police computer expert, C.T. Williams, took three days on the stand to read the salacious pieces of correspondence he uncovered from Michelle's online life, detailing her extramarital affairs and "swinging" experiences. The defense argued the prejudice outweighed any value, but the judge disagreed. This would be the most high-profile case Williams investigated, from the time he started the cyber crimes unit for the department in 1998 until his retirement in 2006, when he opened his own computer forensics firm.

The evidence against Michelle piled up over the course of the thirteen-week trial. She was convicted in December 2004, sentenced to life plus sixteen years for conspiracy.

The appellate court found the evidence "overwhelming," and while agreeing the search for body bags was tenuous evidence, it was only three pages of the five hundred exhibits and twenty-one thousand computer documents, with eighty-eight thousand e-mails and messages; by itself, it wasn't enough to make the trial unfair.

In yet another twist in a case full of turns, in January 2002, more than two years after John Diamond's conviction and months before Michelle's arrest, Diamond's attorney submitted a request for clemency along with a "proffer," an outline of the testimony Diamond could give against Michelle Theer. Military prosecutors had convinced Diamond that he had no reason to continue to protect her.

As author Michael Fleeman said in his book, *The Officer's Wife*, Diamond's proffer gave "a compelling account, the detail so vivid that to read it means never looking at the murder of Marty Theer the same way again."

Diamond said Michelle had threatened to kill her husband for raping her and for trying to kill her with carbon monoxide, that she'd pressured Diamond into getting her a handgun and showing her how to use it. She said she'd never used a handgun in her military training, only an M-16 rifle. Diamond said Michelle was the one who shot Marty the night after the Christmas party.

Diamond parked across Raeford Road from her office, expecting to spend time with her. As he crossed the road, he heard shots and found Marty on the ground with Michelle, wearing surgical gloves, holding the 9mm Diamond had borrowed from a friend when she said she needed protection. She gave him the gun and told him to leave.

The proffer never earned John Diamond any consideration in his sentence, but his version of that December night raises interesting questions about who pulled the trigger near the back stairs that night. He and Michelle both continue to serve life sentences with the possibility of parole.

THE POISONERS

Velma Barfield: The Death Row Granny

"Death Row" or "serial killer" conjure certain images, many created by television, books and movies. None of those images portray North Carolina's Death Row Granny, who defied stereotype and became so well known that, like Cher or Madonna, she became mononymous, known only as "Velma."

Velma Barfield drew attention because so few women commit murder (or are caught and successfully prosecuted)—roughly 10 percent of all murders. When women do kill, on their own and not as the accomplices of violent men, they tend to kill people close to them, people in their care. And they tend to use methods that distance themselves from the crime, that don't require brute force, methods considered sneaky and devious—like poison.

Poison requires trust or intimate access to a victim. Poison is often delivered in food or drink, sometimes in medicine administered to the bedridden and helpless. For all those reasons, murder by poison is commonly considered a "woman's crime." For Velma, the juxtaposition of a matronly mother and a cruel crime naturally drew attention.

One myth about poison, learned from books, movies and television, is that poison can act quickly and painlessly: a sudden gasp, a clutch at the throat, a slump to the floor and it's all done. Nothing could be further from the truth. Poisons that kill immediately don't really exist; cyanide, that well-worn quick exit in spy movies, takes two to five minutes to kill, a long time when a fully conscious brain is terrifyingly aware that the muscles that should power heartbeats and breath are no longer working.

Arsenic, Velma's choice of poisons, is so often associated with murderous death that it is called "inheritance powder." Arsenic is remarkably easy to obtain, even in our more enlightened and regulated times. The proper dosage can be difficult to calculate, and the death can be lingering, painful and messy. And because arsenic is a heavy metal and doesn't degrade or disappear from human tissue over time, bodies exhumed decades later will still contain the arsenic that killed them.

Arsenic is naturally occurring and can be found in drinking water, soil, rice and other plants. Arsenic is not only detectable in tissues decades later but can also preserve tissues. During the Civil War, having loved ones buried on distant battlefields gave added heartache to those who wanted them home; arsenic proved a remarkably effective embalming agent, allowing for those return journeys.

By 1910, arsenic as an embalming agent fell into disfavor, despite its indisputable effectiveness, when people realized it leached from buried bodies and contaminated the groundwater.

Surely, after its long history of unmasked murderers in courts and in mystery novels by the likes of Agatha Christie, no modern-day murderer would consider using arsenic? Ah, but they do. For inexplicable reasons, North Carolina may have hosted more female serial arsenic poisoners than any other state—the ones who got caught, at any rate. Who can say about the ones who weren't caught, in North Carolina or elsewhere?

Why use a poison that doesn't magically disappear from the body, one that can be detected and measured after the body has been safely secreted in the grave for decades? Because it's cheap, easy to obtain and effective.

As one of Eastern North Carolina's female serial poisoners, Velma attracted national interest in the 1970s and 1980s as news of her case shared headlines with another prominent Fayetteville murder case, that of Dr. Jeffrey MacDonald. The MacDonald case took almost a decade to reach a courtroom, but Velma's case moved quickly. Arrested in March 1978, she was convicted in December of that year. She became the first woman sentenced to death in the United States after the reinstatement of the death penalty, and her case became a centerpiece of the national death penalty debate.

Velma was a pleasantly padded, gentle grandmother who crocheted Easter bunny dolls for her grandchildren as her execution date drew nigh and who corresponded with Reverend Billy Graham's wife, Ruth. She'd renewed or deepened her Christian faith and actively ministered to other women in prison. She was known inside as "Mama Margie."

Her case would force nationwide discussions on legal drug use and whether women should be held criminally accountable in the same way men were, but she started life as far from the national spotlight as could be imagined. Born just north of Fayetteville in 1932, the second of nine children, she was sweet and pretty, although she never saw herself that way. She was also frustrated with her life, with the domestic demands of being the oldest daughter and helping care for the family.

In 1949, in the eleventh grade, she found a way out. She started dating Thomas Burke, despite the strictures and curfews placed by her father. Before long, the high school sweethearts had headed across the state line to South Carolina to get married, where no parental permission and no waiting period or blood tests were required. Velma just wanted to leave her house and set out on her own.

She and her mother were afraid to tell her father. The weekend after she eloped, she moved out to live with Thomas and her new in-laws. Velma and Thomas soon had two children, a boy and a girl. Thomas got a job driving a soft drink delivery truck.

Historian and professor David T. Morgan, a Fayetteville native, wrote about meeting Velma. As a young man, he dated one of Thomas Burke's sisters and met Velma at Thomas's parents' house. She held a baby at the time, probably her daughter. Morgan wrote:

> When I first met Velma Barfield, she was Velma Burke, a young mother in her early twenties....I was introduced to this young woman with blond hair, blue eyes, engaging smile, and friendly disposition, although she was shy and bordered on being obsequious. She seemed eager to make a good impression on me, and she did....
>
> The Burkes were good people, and, as far as I could tell, so was Velma. No one could have ever made me believe that twenty-three or twenty-four years later this young mother would be arrested for murdering one man and then subsequently admit to poisoning three other people, including her own mother. Not sweet, flattering, obsequious Velma!

By most accounts, their life settled into a typical small-town pattern—until 1963, when Velma had to get a hysterectomy. The sudden hormone shift and weight gain left her depressed and relying on diet pills, which made her anxious. Then back pain led to a series of prescriptions for pain pills and a growing list of medications. The money needed for new doctors who would write more prescriptions and filling those prescriptions turned this housewife into a check forger.

It was not until Velma's crimes caught up with her that the story behind the story began to emerge—and even then, was that what really happened? When her father drank, he would beat her, her brothers and her mother. Later, she revealed to a criminal psychiatrist, Dorothy Otnow Lewis, and a journalist for the *Village Voice* that her father also sexually abused her. That wasn't something she'd talked about before, not even as part of her defense in court. She'd stayed hurt and angry with her mother for not protecting her. She didn't think women should kowtow to men but should stand up and protect those in their care.

That hurt and sense of abandonment never left Velma, prompting her intense devotion to her children, to the point that she couldn't bear to be separated from them even for short periods, even for a much-anticipated vacation to the North Carolina mountains. As her children became adults, the roles reversed. She wasn't the one protecting her children—she was the one needing protection.

Velma had married quickly, choosing a man who was gentle and kind and, more importantly, someone who would get her away from a father who increasingly was neither of those. Her story didn't end happily ever after. A man drinking and threatening abuse once again became the norm in her own home, reportedly starting after Thomas's father died in 1966. Of course, the financial strain of feeding Velma's increasing appetite for Valium and other drugs couldn't have helped.

Then the unthinkable happened. One April day in 1969, Velma took the children to the laundromat with her. She left Thomas at home in a drunken slumber. While she was gone, their house caught fire, likely caused by a neglected cigarette. Thomas died.

A little more than a year later, in August 1970, Velma married widower Jennings Barfield. She'd worked with his wife at Belk and knew him from his drop-ins at the store. After his wife died, he continued dropping in. Velma could tell he was lonely. He was older, was good company and seemed stable. Their marriage made sense, at first. Six months into the marriage, though, Jennings Barfield was already considering divorce. She'd been bouncing checks on his closed account, and her drug use continued.

In March 1971, Barfield came down with vomiting and diarrhea and quickly died.

By 1974, Velma was keeping company with another man, Al Smith. When he was hit and killed by a car, he left her $5,000 in life insurance, which covered her drug costs for a while. But she still had to move back in with her mother, Lillie Bullard. Velma needed a place to stay, but she resented what felt like a return to the servitude she hated as a teenager.

By the fall, Lillie had developed repeated and escalating bouts of stomach cramps and vomiting. Just after Christmas 1974, she died at the Cape Fear Valley Hospital from gastritis.

With her mother gone, Velma again needed a place to live and a way to support herself, so she began working as a caregiver for an elderly couple, Montgomery Edwards, age ninety-four, and his wife, Dollie, age eighty-four. Montgomery, whose health wasn't good, died in January 1977. Dollie and Velma often quarreled, but Velma continued to work for her until Dollie also became ill with cramps and diarrhea. Dollie was admitted to the hospital and died at the end of February, weeks after her husband's passing.

The following month, Velma found another caregiving job just outside Lumberton, this time with John Henry Lee and his wife, Record. In May, John Henry started suffering from vomiting and diarrhea. He was dead by early June. His wife got sick but survived.

While working for the Lees, Velma began dating Taylor Stuart, the nephew of her former client Dollie Edwards. The relationship was on-again,

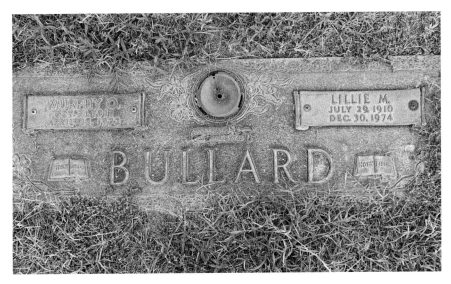

Grave marker for Velma Barfield's mother, a victim Velma had trouble admitting she'd poisoned. *Photo by Cathy Pickens.*

141

off-again, but on January 31, 1978, she moved back in with Stuart. He grew cautious about her after learning she'd once served a three-month sentence for check forgery. She'd also forged checks on his account. Still, Stuart took her back in and even agreed to take her to hear evangelist Rex Humbard's revival in Fayetteville. She was a regular churchgoer, and he knew attending the service would please her. Although she didn't approve of drinking, given her past associations with drunken men, she knew he'd enjoy a beer before they drove to Fayetteville.

He got so sick during the service, he had to excuse himself and lie down in his truck. When she came out of the revival and saw how bad he was, she drove them home. She tried to nurse him at home, but his condition quickly worsened and he had to go to the hospital in Lumberton. Stuart Taylor died in the hospital of gastritis on February 3, 1978, three days after Velma moved back into his house.

His physician couldn't figure out why a healthy man would die so suddenly of a stomach ailment and recommended an autopsy. Stuart's children deferred to Velma, who agreed to the autopsy. On March 6, the toxicology results came back from the lab: arsenic. For the first time, the cycle of illness and death around Velma had an official cause, and it wasn't "bad luck."

No one around her had openly suspected her in any of the deaths. But maybe some had secret suspicions. Soon after the arsenic diagnosis in Taylor Stuart's death, one of Velma's sisters called the Lumberton police from South Carolina and told them about the other deaths that surrounded her.

Police questioned Velma at the station but let her go home. Rumors reached her son Ronnie: police were going to arrest her. He knew she was fragile and that her drug use was out of control. He worried she'd harm herself. He suggested they go back to the police station together.

One officer interviewing her had been in school with Velma; another had been a neighbor kid who played with her son. The officers couldn't quite believe what they were hearing: "I didn't mean to kill him. I only meant to make him sick."

Ronnie asked if she wanted a lawyer. He later regretted not insisting she get one. She seemed to want to tell the story, even though she didn't tell all of it at the time. Some of it she never seemed quite able to admit. She did admit putting Terro Ant Poison in Stuart Taylor's beer and in his tea. Hearing that, county prosecutor Joe Freeman Britt sought exhumations for her mother, Lillie Bullard, for Dollie Edwards and for John Henry Lee. The bodies all contained arsenic.

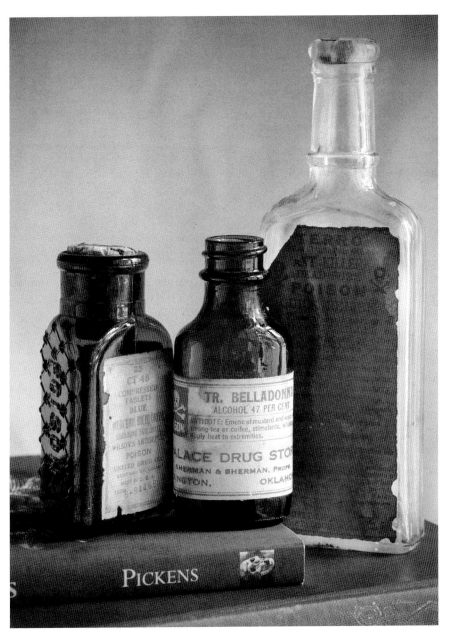

Poison bottles, including arsenic-containing Terro Ant Killer. *Photo by Libby Dickinson.*

When trying first-degree, death penalty–eligible cases, Britt didn't rely on his assistant district attorneys. He insisted on trying those himself.

In 1975, a *Newsweek* article noted that in a seventeen-month period, prosecutor Britt set a "national record for a single prosecutor" in capital murder convictions. He took thirteen first-degree cases to trial and won thirteen death penalties. He was a courtroom legend—dramatic, compelling and a masterful storyteller. As he told *Newsweek*, "You try to re-create just what happened, and you make the jury identify with the victim."

As crime writer Jerry Bledsoe pointed out in his detailed account of the Barfield case, at times Britt's dramatic flair drew criticism, particularly from appellate courts. Susie Sharp, chief justice of the North Carolina Supreme Court, "took the unusual step of publicly upbraiding Britt for his zeal and for courtroom tactics that 'transcended the bounds of propriety and fairness.'" In a rape case, he'd told the jury to note that the defendant's wife hadn't appeared on the stand to support him; Britt didn't point out that spouses weren't allowed to testify. The state Supreme Court overturned that conviction. Britt later admitted that he sometimes got carried away and deserved the criticism.

But the judicial reprimands and overturned verdicts didn't slow Britt down. Bledsoe said, "At one point reporters calculated that of all the people occupying death rows across the country, nearly four percent had been personally put there by Joe Freeman Britt."

Velma was arrested on March 13, 1978, for the poisoning death of her boyfriend (or fiancé, she called him), Stuart Taylor. The process moved quickly. She was convicted later that year, on December 2, by a Bladen County jury and sentenced to death.

On the stand, Velma was combative under Britt's cross-examination, even though, as Kathy Sawyer reported in the *Washington Post*, shedding a few tears—and not arguing with the prosecutor—might have saved her from the death penalty. Velma insisted that she never intended to kill Taylor, or anyone. She would have nursed him back to health, trying to buy herself time to figure out how to repay money she'd taken from his account. That had always been her plan—to make victims sick so she'd have time to repay the money.

The jury debated a little over an hour and found her guilty of first-degree murder. After a tussle in the U.S. Supreme Court over the process by which death penalty verdicts were decided, the death penalty had been reinstated in 1976. In 1983, the North Carolina legislature said that the condemned could choose whether to die in the gas chamber (or by "asphyxia," as Velma's court called it) or by lethal injection. She chose injection.

Bladen County Courthouse in Elizabethtown, site of Velma Barfield's trial. *Photo by Cathy Pickens.*

Her *pro bono* appeals attorney, James D. Little, fought mightily for her, inside the courts and out. Little introduced her to Ellen Schoen, a writer for the *Village Voice*. Schoen came to Raleigh, spent time with Velma in prison and then wrote a front-page article with a provocative headline: "Does This Woman Deserve to Die?: A Grandmother on Death Row." Throughout the series of appeals and delays, Little did everything he could to get local media attention. Now, as Bledsoe described in his book, Little was juggling which national news outlet would get the first interview. The article brought the attention her attorney hoped would save her life.

Her last chance was clemency from the governor. Unfortunately, Governor Jim Hunt was in a dead-heat Senate race with conservative Jessie Helms. Despite national calls for clemency, pointing to her apparently sincere religious conversion and the good work she was doing inside the prison, Hunt couldn't afford to look weak on crime. He refused to halt her execution.

Her much-reported last meal was a Coca-Cola and Cheez Doodles; she wore pink pajamas. She was the first (and so far the last) woman executed in North Carolina since the reinstatement of the death penalty.

Britt, at trial and later, was blunt about how painful death by arsenic is and how deliberate a poisoner has to be in the face of that suffering. Her victims' families worked to give voice to those who'd died, that they not be lost in the push for compassion for Velma. On the other side, Velma's son Ronnie knew the struggle she had with drugs. He'd had to wrestle a tissue full of pills from her hand before he took her to the police station to be interviewed, afraid she'd kill herself. He had worried about an overdose but hadn't believed her capable of murder—until her confession. Even then, he felt sympathy for her struggles.

In the final tally, how many did Velma kill? She later told her son she'd "probably" killed her first husband—his father, Thomas. He was drunk, and she locked the house door when she left, which was odd because they didn't usually lock that door. She might have left a burning cigarette. For some reason, there were crimes she just couldn't bring herself to admit.

Between 1984, when Velma was the first woman executed after 1976, and September 2015, sixteen women were executed in the United States. Twelve were white and four were black. Texas led with four; Florida had two. Of those sixteen women, only two others attracted much national interest or have recognizable names. In 1998, Karla Faye Tucker was the second woman executed; she killed two people with a pickaxe during a robbery, but her religious conversion raised calls for leniency. Aileen Wuornos, executed in Florida in 2002, claimed she'd killed seven men in self-defense while working as a prostitute; Charlize Theron won an Oscar for her portrayal of Wuornos in *Monster*.

Velma's case drew debate for several reasons beyond the relative novelty of female multiple murderers: the debate over drug use and criminal agency; the role of past sexual abuse and of frontal lobe brain injury in criminal behavior; the accelerating debate over the death penalty; considerations of redemption versus punishment in our criminal justice system; how to balance the rights of victims and their families against compassion for the accused; and finally, not insignificantly, the sense that women, as the gentler sex, are less capable of evil and more deserving of forgiveness.

The debate continues, decades after Velma walked into the death chamber wearing her pink pajamas.

Mrs. Ann K. Simpson

If a husband ends up dead, it's best for his wife if she has lived an exemplary life, free of whispers and innuendo. By most accounts, Mrs. Ann K. Simpson had done so. That didn't prevent her from standing trial in 1850, on a Thursday and Friday in November, for the poisoning death of her husband, Alexander Simpson.

Her lead defense attorney told jurors how he'd known Ann when she was a beautiful little girl. Other attorneys—there were six in the case, two prosecuting her and four defending her—spoke of her loveliness, of how terrible it would be if she had her "neck laid bare" for the hangman's noose. Another spoke of how Mr. Simpson had come "from away," gently reminding jurors that Simpson hailed from Esperance, New York. They painted her as a fair flower of southern womanhood.

But other voices were in the courtroom, more refined and less drama-born than the gossip that circled, as gossip would in a small town like Fayetteville when a man dies in agony and two doctors claim he'd been poisoned by arsenic. Those more subdued but damaging courtroom voices repeated the story that Mrs. Simpson told her seamstress, in a moment of duress, about how she'd loved someone else and became engaged to him before she met Simpson and "married him for a home."

That confession, perhaps more girlish and unconsidered than one would expect from a married woman, was prompted by a letter she'd just gotten from her husband: "For the sake of your friends, you may stay in my house but you must find your own clothes as well as you can….You can no longer be my wife."

Overcome as she was by his accusation of infidelity and the orders in the letter that she make him a separate bed, maybe she just had to have someone to talk to and her seamstress's visit that day came at a time where her shock and disbelief overflowed her propriety.

Stories came from other sources too. For at least a year, the Simpsons had kept boarders in their house, so, as was often the case in households in the

1800s, there were witnesses to events that would be far more private in a household operated without servants or boarders.

In addition, Mrs. Simpson regularly visited Mrs. Polly Rising for teacup fortune readings. The fortune-teller reported to a neighbor that Mr. Simpson had struck his wife. The day Mrs. Rising learned that, the fortune she read for Mrs. Simpson noted that Mr. Simpson wouldn't live out the week.

At trial, the prosecutor turned Mrs. Rising's statements against the defendant. Did Mrs. Rising's fortune-telling embolden Mrs. Simpson to do away with her husband? Was "consulting the miserable old hag" not an "idle pastime" but the focus of her passions?

The coroner's jury inquest heard testimony about the death and the postmortem exam and viewed the corpse before announcing it had a spot of trouble lighting on a limb: "[T]hey are inclined to think that the poison was administered by Mrs. Ann K. Simpson, the wife of the deceased. They state, however, that the matter is involved in doubt, and they respectfully refer the whole case to the Superior Court."

The town gossip likely blew even hotter when, before officers of the law could take her into custody that November, Mrs. Simpson "made her escape." She headed to Charleston on her way to Havana, Cuba. A few months later, though, in May 1850, she returned to her hometown to stand trial.

In the days long before 'round-the-clock news and live courtroom video, the public followed criminal trials in pamphlets or broadsides published after the trial. These cheap, popular publications summarized the gruesome details of the murder, the brilliance of the lawyers or detectives and the contrition of the convicted (usually penned by the minister who convinced the condemned of the wisdom of setting things right before the noose fell around him). Later, as the literacy rate increased, newspaper publishers learned that murder sold papers—the more details and drama, the better. Still later, in detailed book-length accounts of the trials, the *Notable British Trials* series set the standard for erudite postmortems of legal proceedings in high-profile trials.

In the United States, similar case reports were published, though not as regularly nor as exhaustive as the British series. The published account of Mrs. Simpson's trial for the arsenic poisoning of her husband runs only 200 pages, with 147 of those pages devoted to the separate closing arguments from five lawyers, including a prosecuting attorney hired by the dead man's family.

The trial focused on two main questions: Did he die of arsenic poisoning? Did she give it to him? The summary of the testimony was succinct. After all, the trial lasted only two days. The facts were straightforward. Ann purchased an ounce of arsenic at Samuel Hinsdale's pharmacy in Fayetteville. Had Mr. Simpson bought any poison himself? The clerk said he didn't personally sell Mr. Simpson any chrome yellow (lead chromium), which causes abdominal pain, seizures and delirium, easily confused with arsenic. The shop did have it for sale, though, as a carriage paint.

In addition, the clerk testified, "I will not say I never sold Mr. Simpson tartar emetic." Tartar emetic, used to purge the stomach of poison or as a treatment for alcohol abuse, was itself poisonous, containing antimony and potassium. Of great importance was the fact that tartar emetic also mimics the effects of arsenic.

Mrs. Simpson had talked openly with others about arsenic, complaining of rats in her house and asking about its effects. She got the kind of ill-informed guidance that comes when asking technical questions of random folks. One of their boarders testified about their dinner conversation on rats. On cross-examination by the defense, he said, "I told her that red arsenic made the rats run to the fire, and that white arsenic makes them take to the water."

Ann also told people she became concerned the arsenic might be dangerous to have around and spread it in the dirt outside to dispose of it.

What foods were eaten, when and by whom are important details to uncover and debate in suspected poisoning cases. The lawyers also focused on exactly when Mr. Simpson first said he didn't feel well and on exactly what fluids came out of him, who observed it and what it meant.

At dinner that November evening, Ann and her husband ate syllabub, a venerable sweet English dessert typically made with lemon juice, cream, sugar and plenty of wine and brandy whipped to a froth. Their boarders did not join them in dessert because both had made temperance pledges. The lawyers in the case much dissected the syllabub. Did she make it because her boarders wouldn't eat it, only she and her husband would? The recipe seems innocuous enough, if you haven't taken a pledge to abstain from alcohol, but what of the other cases around the country where people died after eating syllabub, presumably because of some taint with the wine? The defense lawyers made sure the jurors knew about those other deaths.

She also served coffee after dinner, as was their custom. One boarder said she passed him a cup and then told him it wasn't for him—it was for Mr. Simpson. Was her voice excited, as he suggested? Was it simply that she'd broken with tradition and, instead of first serving the boarder's coffee, first served the sweetened coffee her husband liked? Or was the arsenic in

Collier's drawing by E.W. Kemble, with an illustrated warning about patent medicines in 1905. *Courtesy of Library of Congress, Prints and Photographs Division.*

her husband's coffee? One boarder said Simpson didn't take a second cup because "he felt sick at the stomach."

Arsenic, the inheritance powder famously used by the Borgias in their internecine squabbles, was also routinely used to rid farms and houses of rodents, as well as ants and weeds. Small doses were also used in cosmetics and health tonics.

Fowler's tonic, a 1 percent solution of potassium arsenite, was first marketed in 1786 for ailments as varied as malaria, asthma, psoriasis and general malaise. But it was only one of many tonics containing arsenic and other poisons, as illustrated in editorial cartoons.

Despite its effectiveness in killing off rats and unwanted rivals, arsenic remained widely and generously available until the 1850s, when physicians in England pushed for measures to keep track of it all. Until then, stopping by the pharmacy for arsenic to rid the house or barn of rats was not unlike picking up a can of roach spray or a mousetrap today. It was not until the mid-1850s that British pharmacists began recording arsenic purchases in a "poison book." The Simpson case, though, needed no poison book to prove who bought the arsenic, how much and when—the sales clerk remembered her.

Arsenic was plentiful, but so were diseases with the same symptoms as arsenic poisoning—diseases little known now, thanks to modern medicine. Cholera, caused by waterborne bacteria, can look shockingly like arsenic poisoning: severe diarrhea, nausea and vomiting, dehydration and lethargy, extreme thirst and sometimes seizures. So can gastritis, with its cramps, diarrhea and vomiting.

The doctor testified that Mr. Simpson complained of burning stomach pains, vomiting, diarrhea, cold hands and feet and his "considerable thirst." He had severe symptoms, but what caused them?

One diagnostic of poisoning is the timing of the symptoms compared to the ingestion of suspect food. Arsenic is none too helpful in this respect. The symptoms of arsenic poisoning appear in as little as half an hour or as

Above: *Puck* illustration "The Age of Drugs," with arsenic packets and strychnine bottles in "Kill 'Em Quick Pharmacy." *Courtesy of Library of Congress, Prints and Photographs Division.*

Left: *Puck* 1898 illustration of a doctor with bottles of strychnine, opium, arsenic and calomel (mercury). *Courtesy of Library of Congress, Prints and Photographs Division.*

long as two hours. Severity depends on the dose, but extreme diarrhea is a hallmark. Other symptoms can include a garlic smell on the breath, muscle cramps, severe stomach pains or cramps, confusion and drowsiness.

In poisoning cases, the suspect's behavior is always dissected in detail. Was Ann Simpson's conduct at her husband's sickbed appropriate? No one disputed that she quickly called for the doctor as the diarrhea and vomiting developed. As one lawyer pointed out, poisoners don't typically do that. She stayed by his bed and called for the doctor to return, even calling another doctor to join him—also unusual for a poisoner.

Her every movement and nuance were examined at trial and open to questioning gossip in the street. When she reached out her hand to feel his forehead, he turned away from her. Was he reacting as a man in pain? Or was he withdrawing from the hand that was murdering him? When she said, "Oh, you're a touch-me-not today," was that a gentle joke between spouses? Or a cold-hearted jab? The interpretation depended on whether the lawyer talking was trying to send her to the gallows or save her.

At no time in the trial did an illicit lover appear. None was named, just her single mention of a man she'd known before she married. Perhaps it was understandable that she was wondering "what might have been" after she got the accusatory letter from her husband. Maybe she should have made a different choice, despite her friends' opposition to her first engagement? Or was she assuaging her guilt by confessing to a sympathetic listener her still-harbored feelings for another man? Again, it depends on who was talking.

The bulk of the trial report is devoted not to the analysis of their domestic relations but to the chemical analysis of arsenic. A battle of the almost-experts dominated the trial.

The two physicians in attendance at his death asked Mrs. Simpson's permission to do a postmortem, to confirm what happened. Without hesitation, she agreed—again, unusual for a poisoner. They suspected a heart attack but found his heart undamaged. His stomach and part of the intestine were inflamed. As was recommended practice to preserve the contents for testing, they tied off the digestive tract above and below the inflamed portions and took it away to the lab. They detailed the various tests, which her defense counsel later dissected and even ridiculed.

With speeches pompous and plain, the doctors mostly agreed: Simpson had arsenic in his system. Some of their tests, though, had failed to find it. Others arguably weren't reliable since the doctors had so little actual lab experience.

They also debated whether Mr. Simpson had been poisoned at dinner. In the syllabub or the coffee? Did the timing work out? Or had he taken it himself, perhaps medicinally? On purpose or by accident? Those were difficult questions to answer in any poisoning case in the mid-1800s.

For centuries, arsenic proved a reliable means to eradicate the unwanted because it was cheap, tasteless, colorless, odorless, available, effective... and undetectable. The initial tests for arsenic were discovered by Spaniard Mathieu Orfila, father of toxicology. He supported the "garlic smell test" for arsenic, even though not all forms of arsenic released the odor and detection depended too much on subjective senses and too little on objectively provable measures. By 1830, students studying in London were warned that relying on taste or smell was a suspect method.

The first accurate test for identifying the presence of arsenic in organic material—food or human tissue—was developed in 1832 by English chemist James Marsh. In 1833, Marsh used his new test to show that an elderly local man died from arsenic in his coffee. His grandson, greedy for his estate, was on trial, but jurors didn't find the evidence convincing. Marsh, though, was convinced and continued to share his testing procedures with other chemists and physicians. The Marsh test eventually became state of the art in the 1840 LaFarge poison trial in France. More than a decade after the acquittal in Marsh's first case, Marsh's confidence in his test got added support from an unexpected source: the grandson unexpectedly admitted he'd poisoned his grandfather to get his estate.

For his test, Marsh mixed heated zinc, acid and the suspect substance. If arsenic were present, a silvery coating would be left in the glass. Marsh's test could detect arsenic in long-buried remains and was sensitive enough to detect small amounts accumulated in tissues from long-term poisoning.

Discovering how to detect arsenic in human tissue didn't mean those tests were infallible. The tests could be tricky to conduct and were best done by trained chemists in controlled laboratory settings. Both art and science were required to determine if that silvery deposit was silvery enough.

In 1841, a German chemist added his Reinsch test to the arsenic-detecting arsenal. Reinsch's test couldn't detect the small quantities the Marsh test could, but it was easier to conduct. Two tests were more credible, and procedures became better accepted. Affected organs were routinely removed and sealed in jars. The alimentary canal was tied off above the stomach and at the end of the intestines to preserve the contents—a procedure carefully followed in the Simpson case.

Despite the advances in chemical detection, errors could still occur. Impurities in the testing materials could falsely indicate the presence of arsenic. In one English case, the deceased may have suffered from Crohn's disease rather than arsenic. In another, the culprit may have had Addison's disease. Cholera shares many of the same symptoms, as does severe gastroenteritis. The presence of antimony—the key ingredient in tartar emetic—could easily confuse the test for arsenic.

The lawyers defending Ann Simpson questioned at length the validity of the tests conducted and the capabilities of the doctors and Reverend Dr. Colton. Duncan McRae, the most flowery orator among the lawyers, methodically asked the prosecution's witnesses which learned toxicology texts and authors they recognized as authorities in the field. Then, in his closing argument, McRae quoted at length from those texts. In fact, most of the closing arguments were devoted to analysis, attack and parry about which tests were substantive, what was really proved and what had been called into disfavor within the toxicology community, round and round. McRae, casting aspersions in his closing, said, "You cannot make with bent and broken links a perfect chain."

Of the two "expert" physicians, McRae pointed out that neither had ever been asked to test for arsenic in a body. Neither of them "pretend to any more knowledge in this matter, than such as they have attained from books....They do not pretend to be chemists." Of the testimony of Reverend Dr. Colton, a minister who also trained at Yale in chemistry, McRae said, "[A]ccording to his own estimate of himself would be abundantly sufficient for the prisoner's destruction. But happily for her, if he be judged by other rules, she will be relieved from the danger in which his self-confidence had placed her." Such a pleasant way to slice apart an expert witness and his "sermoniacal lecture on chemistry."

For the jury, McRae spent time analyzing the 1832 Pennsylvania trial of Lucretia Chapman for her husband's poisoning death, where the quality of the testing was also much debated. One chemical expert witness, trained at the Sorbonne and with practical lab experience under noted European academics, found arsenic in the Chapman case by using the garlic "smell test." That expert was a young Thomas G. Clemson, later founder of Clemson University. Mrs. Chapman was acquitted; her lover was convicted.

McRae ridiculed the smell and color tests: "Is human life so cheap that it may be sacrificed upon a shade of color?" And it was "bad enough that the government should have sought the prisoner's life" using the colors observed in the physicians' tests, but smells too? Even after Dr. Colton admitted himself that his nose didn't work well any longer? On that basis Mrs. Simpson stood trial? McRae's indignation leaps from the transcript. His voice in that courtroom would have sounded more dramatically indignant than printed words can convey.

While taking courtly pains to commend the opposing counsel and the prosecution's expert witnesses, McRae and Mrs. Simpson's defense team didn't, according to the record, call experts of their own, relying instead on cross-examining the prosecution experts and on using the recognized textbooks to discredit them, to belittle their experience and to call attention to the weaknesses inherent in arsenic analysis in the hands of the inexperienced.

Did the jury pay much real attention to the technical debate? Arsenic was found, but how did it get in his body? Did she poison him? Little evidence surfaced that she did. After all, no one *saw* her put poison in his syllabub or coffee. Her attorneys offered credible arguments of accidental poisoning (by referring to other deaths, of which the jury apparently would have been familiar) or even by self-administration (in a tonic or solution he had purchased himself, rather than by an attempt to commit suicide, although that too was broached).

In the end, who knows what the jurors considered most important. A sympathetic local woman? Too much dizzying scientific information to digest? No clear-cut evidence that she'd been unfaithful to her husband, only that he'd accused her and struck her? No clear-cut advantage in getting him out of the way? No "other man" ever materialized; she sat in court every day with her mother.

In the end, after listening to five lengthy summations of the testimony from five able attorneys, the jury of twelve men took three hours to find Mrs. Simpson not guilty.

Of North Carolina's parade of famous female poisoners—Velma, Nannie Doss, Blanche Taylor Moore, Ann Miller—Ann Simpson is the only one accused but not convicted of poisoning her husband. There her story fades from our view.

SIDE TRIPS, CRIME BITS
AND ODDITIES

Eastern North Carolina has its own special affinities when it comes to combining crime with quirkiness.

For starters, Eastern North Carolina unexpectedly hosted at least two famous mummies. One began hanging out in the McDougald Funeral Home in Laurinburg in 1911. Cancetto Farmica, as he was known in life, was a traveling carnival worker. According to the story, during a carnival stop in McColl, South Carolina, he and a coworker got in a fight. Cancetto's head got a solid blow from a tent stake; he got a horse and buggy ride to the hospital in Laurinburg, where he died.

Farmica and his father were recent immigrants from Italy. His father, traveling with another carnival, came to Laurinburg and put down ten dollars toward the embalming, all the money he could afford. He made a very specific request: the family wanted the body returned to Italy so it could only be buried in consecrated ground at a Catholic cemetery. After the family got the bill, they apparently couldn't come up with the money and never got in contact again.

Unfortunately, it wasn't uncommon for funeral homes to have on-premises bodies with outstanding bills whose families couldn't afford to lay them to rest. It also wasn't uncommon for "mummies" to travel on display with carnivals. Maybe inspired by Farmica's past life with the carnival, he became a popular display at the funeral home and appeared on local, national and international television programs. Journalist Tim Bullard remembered, as a boy, first seeing the mummy in a box in the funeral home garage.

Maybe it was his local nickname, "Spaghetti," or increasing sensitivities as time passed, but in 1972, a New York politician of Italian descent took up Spaghetti/Farmica's cause, calling the treatment disrespectful. The McDougalds arranged for a Catholic service, presided over by a priest from Hamlet. Journalist Bullard said two hundred people attended the funeral service.

Farmica would be an interesting story on his own, but he wasn't Eastern North Carolina's only carnival mummy. Farmica didn't travel; he just hung around the funeral home. Marie O'Day, on the other hand, took to the road.

Marie's legend billed her as a saloon singer, stabbed to death by her husband in the 1920s and pickled in the Great Salt Lake in Utah. She then began her postmortem traveling life with other carnival classics like Gorilla Girl, until she ended her show business run stored in a shed in Wilson, North Carolina, after the carnival stopped operating.

In 2002, professors Jerry Conlogue and Ron Beckett, hosting *The Mummy Road Show*, investigated Marie's story to separate fact from carnival hype—and found that her famous "story" was mostly hype. To provide a good draw as a carnival sideshow, a mummy needed a spine-tingling backstory. Unlikely that many people would have paid to see Marie's remains had the story been "she died of pneumonia, no one claimed her, and arsenic embalming fluid is a fantastically effective preservative."

The carnival owner advertised to sell her, along with his other curiosities, when he retired from the road. The cable TV show *American Pickers* paid her a visit. Last reports were that her remains were still stored in a Wilson warehouse. Online commenters wonder why no one has liberated her and given her a proper burial.

Eastern North Carolina seems to have more than its share of misplaced remains, and not all abandoned bodies were first beautifully and thoroughly embalmed and ready to be viewed by paying audiences and the macabrely curious. In one case, the body was folded into a freezer.

In some ways, the 2016 case in Goldsboro defies logic. It's conceivable that someone relying on a mother's benefit check would not like to see those payments come to an end. Fear of financial difficulties is understandable. In a panic, a daughter might stuff her dead mother into a large, deep freezer. In a panic, she might later not know how to undo that decision.

The less-comprehensible part comes when the fifty-six-year-old daughter decided to sell the freezer to her neighbor. The sale had a condition: the daughter told the buyer someone was coming to pick up the contents for a church "time capsule," so would she please not open the freezer or mess with the contents until the Sunday school class members came to get it? At thirty dollars, the freezer was a bargain, so the buyer agreed to the condition and left it running in her back bedroom, with its duct tape seal.

After three weeks, the new owner got tired of waiting. When she untaped the lid and opened it, she told a news reporter, she found a sheet, a bag of kitty litter and a human foot.

Even the *Washington Post* reported on the unusual find, along with the post-autopsy revelations that the woman died of natural causes and that police were looking for the daughter for failure to report a death.

The question persists though: Why sell the freezer? Then again, what does one do with a freezer with a body inside?

Bootlegger's Daughter

We long to solve mysteries, and we want the solutions to be worthy of their mysteries. Sometimes, though, the ending is so unexpected as to be… ordinary. Tragic, but not so mysterious, once the story is told.

In 1993, native North Carolinian Margaret Maron won the Mystery Writers of America's prestigious Edgar Award for her novel *Bootlegger's Daughter*. In Maron's novel, she offered a fictional resolution to a sadly unsolved murder in Johnston County.

In December 1972, Bonnie Neighbors left home in Benson, North Carolina, to pick up her seven-year-old son from school. She had her four-month-old son with her when she disappeared. Just as in Maron's novel, the beautiful young mother was found dead with her still-alive son next to her. She had been bound and shot.

Few expected the real-life case to be solved, especially after forty-seven years. Few anticipated the tragic ordinariness of its ending.

Bonnie Neighbors's murder became one of those cases solved by a combination of tenacious police work and increasingly sophisticated DNA technology.

In May 2019, Larry Joe Scott, age sixty-five, was arrested in Bradenton, Florida. Scott was a drifter, and the crime was random. The case had been passed from one sheriff to the next over the decades, evidence of the difficulty and frustration in solving homicides committed by strangers. Sheriff Steve Bizzell was fourteen years old when Bonnie Neighbors was killed. The press conference announcing Scott's cold-case arrest made clear how much the case had haunted Bizzell and other investigators. According to Attorney General Josh Stein, the state crime lab performed forty-seven tests on material in the case between 1972 to 1999.

Stories need endings, no matter how long it takes or how sad the ending remains.

The Lost Colony

Miniaturist painter John White signed on with Sir Walter Raleigh's 1587 expedition to plant England's first colony in North America. Sixteenth-century ocean voyages were dangerous. Among the more than one hundred passengers, in cramped, disease-encouraging confines, traveled White's wife, daughter and son-in-law.

The Spanish, with their naval strength, commanded the Caribbean waters and much of the North and South American coasts. This small English group slipped its ship inside North Carolina's barrier islands and settled on Roanoke Island, somewhat protected from both weather and patrolling Spanish galleons.

Over the next months, a drought affected the natives' ability to feed themselves, much less continue to aid the newcomers. John White soon had to leave his daughter and newborn granddaughter and sail to England seeking supplies and support.

White found himself in a perfect storm—not of weather but of war, politics and financial turbulence—that prevented him from raising funds, getting provisions or even finding a ship for passage back to Roanoke Island.

In 1590, White finally dropped anchor off the island, where they saw smoke from a large fire. A signal? They couldn't get through the coastal growth to the source. They investigated both ends of the island. No one came onto the beach to greet them.

Eventually, White got a bit of reassurance when they found *CROATOAN* carved into a post or tree. That had been the agreed-on signal should the settlement have to relocate. White was relieved not to see a cross carved with the word, which would have indicated they were in distress when they left. The message meant they'd moved to Croatoan—today, known as Hatteras Island—and they weren't in trouble when they left.

That was all John White knew—or would ever know with certainty about his daughter and his granddaughter, Virginia Dare. Virginia would have

Croatoan carving on Roanoke Island. *Courtesy of the Miriam and Ira D. Wallach Division of Art, Prints and Photographs: Picture Collection, New York Public Library.*

been a toddler when he returned with supplies, assuming she'd beaten the odds of infant mortality. He had to sail home. He never saw or got word of them again.

A father in 1590 would be like any father. The "past" for us was his painful "now." Watching Roanoke Island—and the colony he'd planned—disappear behind him had to be wrenching.

Before and after what became known as the Lost Colony, lots of early settlers in the New World disappeared or were taken in by indigenous settlements. Speculation about the fate of Virginia Dare, though, has ignited musing and investigation for more than four hundred years. Who wouldn't wonder what happened to a little girl we know by name, the first baby born of English settlers in the New World, whose family felt her loss along with the end of what started as a dream of prosperity and hope?

Andrew Lawler, in his 2018 book, *The Secret Token: Myth, Obsession, and the Search for the Lost Colony of Roanoke*, explored the history and speculation around the enduring mystery. The theories have run the gamut from death (either from disease or starvation or predation) to assimilation into one of the tribes who'd offered help and advice to the colonists to, oddly enough, aliens or zombies.

In a 2014 book, author Scott Huler wrote of retracing in modern times the journey John Lawson took in 1700 from Charleston to the Roanoke

Island area. Lawson traveled those lands a little more than one hundred years after the colony was last seen. The story told to him in 1700 was simple: the settlers had gone to Croatoan. Natives who'd been friendly to them were living there, and they could eat from the sea during a time when crops didn't take.

The solution was logical. But we still love a mystery.

Pirates

In exploring crime in the coastal region, among the earliest and most colorful would be the pirate bands that pillaged ships along the coast until the mid-1720s. While North Carolina trade suffered from the lack of a deep-water port, it thrived as a haven for pirates, thanks to the inlets and waterways that provided enviable places in which to hide a fleet from searchers or from which to mount an ambush.

As the European naval powers battled for sea supremacy, the coast of North Carolina was only one of the sites of their sorties and battles—but one of the most active. In those days, the line between being a pirate liable to hang for your crimes and a privateer doing the bidding of your monarch could be perilously fine. Depending on the whims or ouster of his monarch, a legal privateer could quickly become a hunted pirate.

Of those who made no bones about their criminal independence in this time of mercurial allegiances, the name Blackbeard stands out. Research suggests that Edward Teach, a version of Blackbeard's birth name, was a master of public relations and personal branding. Those fearsome tales and woodcuts showing his blazing eyes, his head wreathed in eerie smoke from lighted squibs stuck in his hat, are enduring images of Blackbeard, but he was neither the most effective nor the most brutal of the pirates. Baylus Brooks, a maritime historian, believes he has uncovered Blackbeard's family roots and offers an unexpected portrait. Turns out that Teach was likely an educated man, a member of a Jamaican planter family from Bristol, England. Along with rum, guns and valuables, Blackbeard reportedly helped himself to books onboard captured ships—not stereotypical loot for a vicious pirate.

He sailed only two years before his fatal battle in 1718 at Ocracoke Inlet. Captain Charles Johnson's *A General History of the Pyrates*, a book once credited to Daniel Defoe of *Robinson Crusoe* fame, is the source of what became Blackbeard's swashbuckling legend.

Edward Teach, or Blackbeard, as illustrated in *A General History of the Pyrates*. *Courtesy of Project Gutenberg.*

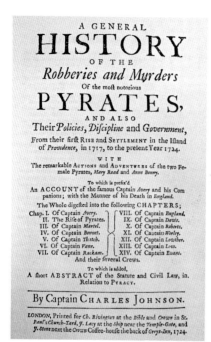

Left: Frontispiece of Captain Charles Johnson's definitive book on "pyrates," often credited to Daniel Defoe. *Courtesy of Project Gutenberg.*

Right: A ghoul welcomes visitors to Grave Digger's Dungeon, a roadside attraction in Currituck County. *Photo by Cathy Pickens.*

Any region that began with the mystery of the Lost Colony and had Blackbeard as one of its first "criminals," along with the gentleman pirate Stede Bonnet and female pirates Mary Read and Anne Bonny, certainly has stories worth telling.

REFERENCES

Black Widow I

Fimrite, Peter. "Marin County: Police Seek Local Victims of Alleged 'Black Widow.'" *SFGate*, July 6, 2007. https://www.sfgate.com/bayarea/article/MARIN-COUNTY-Police-seek-local-victims-of-2553566.php.

Miller, Eric, and Skip Hollandsworth. "The Black Widow." *D Magazine* (May 1987). http://www.dmagazine.com/publications/d-magazine/1987/may/the-black-widow.

Murphy, Dennis. "Widow Leaves Trail of Murder and Suicide." *Dateline NBC* transcript, August 6, 2007.

Rehrig, Gloria. Personal reflections on her trip to North Carolina, dated March 6, 2008.

Whitley, Glenna. "Black (Eyed) Widow." *D Magazine* (August 1990). http://www.dmagazine.com/publications/d-magazine/1990/august/black-eyed-widow.

———. "Black Widow Pleads Guilty." *Dallas Observer*, February 28, 2008. https://www.dallasobserver.com/news/black-widow-pleads-guilty-6406079.

———. "Fall of the Black Widow." *Dallas Observer*, March 8, 2007. www.dallasobserver.com/2007-03-08/news/fall-of-the-black-widow.

———. "Fatal Web: The Arrest of Dallas' 'Black Widow' Lights a Fire under Cold Murder Case." *Dallas Observer*, June 21, 2007. http://www.dallasobserver.com/2007-06-21/news/fatal-web/full.

———. "Seductress of the Saints." *Dallas Observer*, December 9, 2004. https:// www.dallasobserver.com/news/seductress-of-the-saints-6383321.

———. "Whatever Happened to the Black Widow: Sandra Bridewell." *D Magazine* (May 1989). https://www.dmagazine.com/publications/d-magazine/1989/May/whatever-happened-to-the-black-widow-Sandra-Bridewell. Additional articles from Whitley will be organized chronologically following.

Undetermined

Buff, Elaine. *Out with Three: The Murder and Betrayal of Bald Head Island Police Officer Davina Buff Jones*. N.p.: privately published, 2007.

Buff v. N.C. Law Enforcement Offices, I.C. Nos. 980154 LH-0286 (N.C. Indus. Comm. 2005), June 27, 2005.

Charlotte Observer. "Panel Agrees Officer Did Not Kill Herself." July 4, 2005, 4B.

Dittrich, Stacy. "Analysis of 13-Year Mysterious Death of Cape Fear Police Woman." Forbes.com, June 25, 2012. https://www.forbes.com/sites/crime/2012/06/25/analysis-of-13-year-mysterious-death-of-cape-fear-police-woman/#191140596ebd.

Gonzales, Jason, and Julian March. "DA: Bald Head Officer's 1999 Death Not Definitively Suicide." *Star News Online*, December 17, 2013. https://www.starnewsonline.com/article/NC/20131217/News/605048563/WM.

Griffin, Anna. "Bald Head Island Mystery: Murder or Suicide?" *Charlotte Observer*, June 2, 2002, 1A, 12A–13A.

Rhew, Adam. "Shadows by the Sea." *Charlotte Magazine* (March 19, 2014). http://www.charlottemagazine.com/Charlotte-Magazine/April-2014/Shadows-by-the-Sea.

2017 Stats of the State of North Carolina. National Center for Health Statistics, Centers for Disease Control and Prevention. https://www.cdc.gov/nchs/pressroom/states/northcarolina/northcarolina.htm.

WWAY News. "Suicide Death of Davina Buff Jones Now Ruled 'Undetermined.'" December 17, 2013. https://www.wwaytv3.com/2013/12/17/suicide-death-of-davina-buff-jones-now-ruled-undetermined.

The Missing and the Missed

Bomar, Horace L., Jr. "The Lindbergh Law." *Law and Contemporary Problems* 1 (1934): 435–44. https://scholarship.law.duke.edu/lcp/vol1/iss4/5.

Breed, Allen G. "Finding Bobby Dunbar." *Tulsa World*, February 1, 2004. https://www.tulsaworld.com/archive/finding-bobby-dunbar/article_459ff998-f2b9-5f68-adf9-841504ec4910.html.

Charlotte Observer. "Boy May Yet Be Found." September 7, 1906.

———. "Harrison Admitted Deed: Witnesses Tell of Confession." March 16, 1907.

———. "Harrison Out on Bond." September 11, 1906.

Fass, Paula. "Child Kidnapping in America." *Current Events in Historical Perspective*, January 2010. http://origins.osu.edu/article/child-kidnapping-america.

McThenia, Tal, and Margaret Dunbar Cutright. *A Case for Solomon: Bobby Dunbar and the Kidnapping that Haunted a Nation.* New York: Free Press, 2012.

Oldham, Charles. *The Senator's Son: The Shocking Disappearance, the Celebrated Trial, and the Mystery that Remains a Century Later.* North Chesterfield, VA: Beach Glass Books, 2018.

Raleigh News & Observer. "Harrison Denies Guilt; in His Cell the Convicted Kidnapper Protests His Innocence." March 24, 1907, 34.

Ross, Christian K. *The Father's Story of Charley Ross, the Kidnapped Child.* Philadelphia, PA: Potter & Company, 1876.

State v. Harrison, 145 N.C. 408, 59 S.E.2d 867 (NC Sup Ct 1907).

Washington Times. "DNA Clears Up 1914 Case." May 5, 2004. https://www.washingtontimes.com/news/2004/may/5/20040505-111755-3134r.

Wellman, Manly Wade. "Where Are You, Kenneth Beasley?" In *Dead and Gone: Classic Crimes of North Carolina.* Chapel Hill: University of North Carolina Press, 1954.

Black Widow II

Barr, Suzanne. *Fatal Kiss.* Cape Coral, FL: Write Stuff, 2005.

Basden v. Lee, 290 F.3d 602 (4th Cir. 2002).

Deadly Sins. "Small Town Massacre." Investigation Discovery, first aired February 9, 2013.

Gaub, Adam, and Jason O. Boyd. "Parole Board Hears Case for Twice-Convicted Lenoir County Woman." *New Bern News*. https://wcti12.com/news/local/parole-board-hears-case-for-twice-convicted-lenoir-county-woman.

Leland, Elizabeth. "Death Stalks North Carolina Family." *Chicago Tribune*, December 18, 1992. https://www.chicagotribune.com/news/ct-xpm-1992-12-18-9204250310-story.html.

Scene of the Crime with Tony Harris. "Death of a Salesman." Investigation Discovery, first aired July 1, 2018.

Smith, Barry. "Death Penalty Opponents Decry Basden's Fate." *New Bern Sun Journal*, November 20, 2002.

State v. White, 340 N.C. 264, 457 S.E.2d 841 (1995).

Unknownmisandry. "Sylvia Ipock-White, North Carolina Black Widow Serial Killer—1992." Blog, May 20, 2014. http://unknownmisandry.blogspot.com/2014/sylvia-ipock-white-north-carolina-black.html.

Wilson Daily Times. "Dentist Charged with Wife's Murder." November 27, 1992, 4A.

Bad Science

Terri Henson

Forensic Files. "Fire Dot Com." Season 6, Episode 6, aired June 25, 2001.

Grann, David. "Trial by Fire: Did Texas Execute an Innocent Man?" *The New Yorker*, September 7, 2009. https://www.newyorker.com/magazine/2009/09/07/trial-by-fire.

Hansen, Mark. "Badly Burned: Long-Held Beliefs About Arson Science Have Been Debunked after Decades of Misuse and Scores of Wrongful Convictions." *ABA Journal* (December 2015): 36–43.

Humes, Edward. *Burned*. New York: Dutton, 2019.

Hurst, Gerald. Investigative report for arson defendant Terri Hinson. Truth in Justice, March 16, 1998. http://www.truthinjustice.org/hurstrept.htm.

Interview with Gerald Hurst. PBS *Frontline* and WGBH TV, January 15, 2010. https://www.pbs.org/wgbh/pages/frontline/death-by-fire/interviews/gerald-hurst.html#1.

Lentini, John J. "Indicators of Trouble." Fire Scientist. http://www.firescientist.com/Documents/IndicatorsOfTrouble.pdf.

Saker, Anne. "Terri's Fire." Eight-part series. Truth in Justice. http://www.truthinjustice.org/terri1.htm.

Zeak, Tim. "Myths and Other Falsehoods Are Often Presented as Scientific Evidence." Truth in Justice. http://www.truthinjustice.org/arson-myths.

Louise Robbins

Ahearn, Lorraine. "Anthropologist Testified Nationwide; Greensboro Trial Expert a Charlatan, CBS Says." *Greensboro News & Record*, May 12, 1992. https://www.greensboro.com/anthropologist-testified-nationwide-greensboro-trial-expert-a-charlatan-cbs-says/article_8c46b2ab-0521-5664-a78e-43032cdf51e8.html.

Fisher, Jim. "Dr. Louise Robbins: The Shoe Print Expert from Hell." *Jim Fisher True Crime Blog*, February 26, 2018. http://jimfishertruecrime.blogspot.com/2012/03/dr-louise-robbins-shoe-print-expert.html.

Frye v. U.S., 293 Fed. 1013 (D.C. Cir. 1923). The *Frye* holding was modified in the 1993 Supreme Court case of *Daubert v. Merrell Dow Pharmaceuticals*, 509 U.S. 579 (1993). *Daubert* required five elements for a new scientific technique: (1) can be and has been tested; (2) subjected to peer review and publication; (3) established known or potential error rate; (4) standards control its operation; and (5) widespread acceptance within a relevant scientific community. Judges still serve as gatekeepers preventing experts from testifying to scientific methods that don't meet the *Daubert* test.

Hansen, Mark. "Believe It Or Not." *ABA Journal* (June 1993): 64–67.

Mahany, Barbara. "Expert Witness' Expertise on Trial." *Chicago Tribune*, August 18, 1986. https://www.chicagotribune.com/news/ct-xpm-1986-08-18-8603010648-story.html.

Robbins, Louise. *Footprints: Collection, Analysis, and Interpretation*. Springfield, IL: Charles C. Thomas, 1985.

State v. Bullard, 312 N.C. 129, 322 S.E.2d 370 (1984).

The Rockingham Murders

Cole/Ormond Case

Bridges, Myrtle N. *The Shadow of Bill: A Tragic Love Story of Bill & Libbut*. N.p.: privately published, 2015. http://www.myrtlebridges.us/shadowbill.html. Thanks to the research efforts of Myrtle N. Bridges, the regional news articles covering this case are collected in her book, making it possible for readers to see the story unfold as readers saw it in 1925, with the benefit of several reportorial points of view.

Hutchinson, John. *Watch My Smoke: The Cotton Mill Owner Who Got Away with Murder.* N.p.: privately published, 2019.

Mr. Lincoln and New York. "Daniel Sickles (1819–1914)." Gilder Lehrman Institute of American History. http://www.mrlincolnandnewyork.org/new-yorkers/daniel-sickles-1819-1914.

Pickens, Cathy. *Charleston Mysteries.* Charleston, SC: The History Press, 2007, 134–42.

Bob Hines Case

Gogineni, Rama Rao, MD, and Thomas Newmark, MD. "Pseudologia Fantastica: A Fascinating Case Report." *Psychiatric Annals* 44, no. 10 (2014). https://www.healio.com/psychiatry/journals/psycann/2014-10-44-10/%7B930cc27f-9c1f-4f4c-b533-2ae16b8fb153%7D/pseudologia-fantastica-a-fascinating-case-report.

Hart, Reese. "Old Unsolved Cases Still Haunt SBI." *Charlotte Observer*, March 9, 1964, 38.

Mozingo, Barbara. *The 1939 Unsolved Murder of Bob Hines in Richmond County, North Carolina.* Columbia, SC: Alexander Milligan, 2014.

Swamp Outlaws

Fold3. "Henry Berry Lowrie & The Lumbee—Stories." October 17, 2008. https://www.fold3.com/page/3545-henry-berry-lowrie-the-lumbee/stories.

Leland, Elizabeth. "The Land of Legend: Robeson County's Grave Markers and Cypress Swamps Tell Tale of Infamous Lumbee Indian Outlaw." *Charlotte Observer*, June 16, 2002, 1G.

Lowery, Malinda Maynor. *The Lumbee Indians: An American Struggle.* Chapel Hill: University of North Carolina Press, 2018.

Oakley, Christopher Arris. "The Legend of Henry Berry Lowry: *Strike at the Wind!* and the Lumbee Indians of North Carolina." *Mississippi Quarterly* 60, no. 1 (Winter/Spring 2007): 59–80.

Townsend, George Alfred. *The Swamp Outlaws.* New York: R.M. DeWitt, 1872.

Unprecedented

Loftus, Dr. Elizabeth, and Katherine Ketcham. *Witness for the Defense: The Accused, the Eyewitness, and the Expert Who Puts Memory on Trial*. New York: St. Martin's Griffin, 1992.

North Carolian Superior Court Judges' Benchbook. North Carolina Rules of Evidence 403. https://benchbook.sog.unc.edu/sites/default/files/pdf/Rule%20403%20Mar%202015.pdf.

Patterson, Thom. "Triple Murder Suspect Goes from Guilty to Innocent and Back to Guilty." *CNN*, July 18, 2014. https://www.cnn.com/2014/07/18/us/death-row-stories-hennis/index.html.

Schmidle, Nicholas. "Three Trials for Murder." *The New Yorker*, November 14, 2011. https://www.newyorker.com/magazine/2011/11/14/three-trials-for-murder.

State v. Hennis, 323 N.C. 279, 372 S.E.2d 523 (N.C. Sup. Ct. 1988).

U.S. v. Hennis. U.S. Army Court of Criminal Appeals, ARMY 20100304, October 6, 2016. https://www.courtlistener.com/pdf/2016/10/06/united_states_v._master_sergeant_timothy_b._hennis.pdf.

Whisnant, Scott. *Innocent Victims*. New York: Onyx True Crime, 1993.

Online Swingers and a Shooter

Fleeman, Michael. *The Officer's Wife*. New York: St. Martin's, 2006.

State of North Carolina v. Theer. Court of Appeals of North Carolina, No. COA05-1640, January 16, 2007.

Thrasher, Alice. "Technological Private Eye Finds What Computer Lost." *Fayetteville Observer*, January 30, 2008. http://www.crimeresearch.org/articles/computer_lost.

Tresniowski, Alex. "Makeover Madness." *People*, October 14, 2002. https://people.com/archive/makeover-madness-vol-58-no-16.

U.S. v. Diamond. United States Army Court of Appeals, ARMY 20010761, December 21, 2007.

WRAL-TV. "Air Force Widow Convicted of Murder Punished for Escape." Mary 17, 2010. https://www.wral.com/news/local/story/7616559.

———. "Judge: Prosecutors Can Use Computer Evidence in Their Case." July 21, 2004. https://www.wral.com/news/local/story/112357.

Television

Dateline NBC. "Deadly Triangle." First aired October 29, 2010.

Killer Couples. "Michelle Theer and John Diamond." Season 8, Episode 5, Oxygen, first aired September 3, 2016.

Sins and Secrets. "Fayetteville." Season 2, Episode 3, first aired January 26, 2012.

Snapped. "Michelle Theer." Season 3, Episode 14, first aired April 30, 2006.

The Poisoners

Barfield v. Woodard, 748 F.2d 844 (4th Cir. 1984). Federal *habeas* and stay of execution appeal.

Bledsoe, Jerry. *Death Sentence: The True Story of Velma Barfield's Life, Crimes and Execution.* New York: Dutton, 1998.

Celebrated Trials of All Countries. "Trial of Lucretia Chapman." Philadelphia, PA: E.L. Carey and A. Hart, 1835.

Haigh, William H. *The Trial of Mrs. Ann K. Simpson, Charged with the Murder of her Husband, Alexander C. Simpson, by Poisoning with Arsenic.* Fayetteville, NC: Edward J. Hale & Son, 1851.

Hughes, Michael F., et al. "Arsenic Exposure and Toxicology: A Historical Perspective." *Toxicological Sciences* (July 12, 2011): 305–32.

Johns Hopkins Center for Health Security. Cyanide Fact Sheet, December 1, 2003. http://www.centerforhealthsecurity.org/our-work/publications/cyanide-fact-sheet.

Morgan, David T. *Murder Along the Cape Fear: A North Carolina Town in the Twentieth Century.* Macon, GA: Mercer University Press, 2005, 148–80.

Sawyer, Kathy. "Tears Might Have Eased Penalty." *Washington Post*, October 21, 1984. https://www.washingtonpost.com/archive/politics/1984/10/21/tears-might-have-eased-penalty/2dfae8cb-b1d1-477a-afba-c7d4ca62921b/?utm_term=.65a5b9eea3b1.

Schupack, Debbie. "42 Killers Sentenced to Die: Tenacious North Carolina Prosecutor Builds His Life on Death." *Los Angeles Times.* https://www.latimes.com/archives/la-xpm-1986-06-29-mn-373-story.html.

State of North Carolina v. Margie Bullard Barfield, 298 N.C. 306, 259 S.E.2d 510 (1979). State appeal.

Thorwald, Jürgen. *The Century of the Detective.* New York: Harcourt, Brace, 1965. Translated from the German by Richard and Clara Winston.

Wellman, Manly Wade. "Arsenic and Fayetteville." In *Dead and Gone: Classic Crimes of North Carolina*. Chapel Hill: University of North Carolina Press, 1954, 23–42.

Whorton, James C. *The Arsenic Century*. New York: Oxford University Press, 2010.

Wolfe, Linda. *The Murder of Dr. Chapman*. New York: HarperCollins, 2004.

Side Trips, Crime Bits and Oddities

Bullard, Tim. "Spaghetti Hung Around Laurinburg a Long Time." *SCNow Morning News*, February 11, 2013. https://www.scnow.com/news/article_1c1d6d4c-7478-11e2-a34a-0019bb30f31a.html.

Cordingly, David. Introduction in Captain Charles Johnson's *A General History*. Guilford, CT: Lyons Press, 1998, 2010.

Huler, Scott. *A Delicious Country: Rediscovering the Carolinas Along the Route of John Lawson's 1700 Expedition*. Chapel Hill: University of North Carolina Press, 2019.

Johnson, Captain Charles. *A General History of the Pyrates*. London, 1724.

Johnson, Joe. "Her Body Was Found with Her Baby, Still Alive, Beside Her. 47 Years Later, an Arrest." *Raleigh News & Observer*, April 30, 2019. https://www.newsobserver.com/news/local/article229848629.html#storylink=cpy.

Lawler, Andrew. *The Secret Token: Myth, Obsession, and the Search for the Lost Colony of Roanoke*. New York: Anchor Books, 2018.

———. "Three Centuries After His Beheading, a Kinder, Gentler Blackbeard Emerges." *Smithsonian Magazine* (November 13, 2018). https://www.smithsonianmag.com/history/three-centuries-after-his-beheading-kinder-gentler-blackbeard-emerges-180970782/#mc9VRkjcMQFCoe36.99.

Sideshow World. "Marie O'Day." http://www.sideshowworld.com/76-Blow/Marie/Main/Page-O%27Day.html.

Wang, Yanan. "Body in Yard-Sale Freezer Freaks Out N.C. Woman. But then She Recognized the Foot." *Washington Post*, June 2, 2016. https://www.washingtonpost.com/news/morning-mix/xp/2016/06/02/woman-freaked-out-to-find-body-in-yard-sale-freezer-the-foot-tells-the-tale.

Washburn, Mark. "N.C. Mummy Mystery Is Unraveled." *Charlotte Observer*, November 30, 2002, 9F.

ABOUT THE AUTHOR

Cathy Pickens, a lawyer and college professor, is a crime fiction writer (*Southern Fried Mysteries*, St. Martin's/Minotaur) and true crime columnist for *Mystery Readers Journal*. She taught law in the McColl School of Business and served as provost at Queens University of Charlotte and as national president of Sisters in Crime and on the boards of Mystery Writers of America and the Mecklenburg Forensic Medicine Program (an evidence collection/preservation training collaborative). She is also the author of *CREATE!* (ICSC Press), offers workshops on developing the creative process, coaches and teaches new writers through Charlotte Lit and works with former inmates on starting their own businesses and writing their own stories. Also from The History Press: *Charleston Mysteries* and *Charlotte True Crime Stories*.

Visit us at
www.historypress.com